7199

818.5
F

Fuller, Edmund, 1914-
   Successful calamity; a writer's follies on a
Vermont farm.   New York, Random House [1966]
   239p.   21cm.

1. Vermont. 2. Farm life-Vermont.   I. Title.

RBP

Successful Calamity

BOOKS BY EDMUND FULLER

A PAGEANT OF THE THEATRE

JOHN MILTON

A STAR POINTED NORTH (NOVEL)

BROTHERS DIVIDED (NOVEL)

GEORGE BERNARD SHAW: *Critic of Western Morale*

VERMONT: *A History of the Green Mountain State*

TINKERS AND GENIUS: *The Story of the Yankee Inventors*

MAN IN MODERN FICTION

BOOKS WITH MEN BEHIND THEM

THE CORRIDOR (NOVEL)

SUCCESSFUL CALAMITY

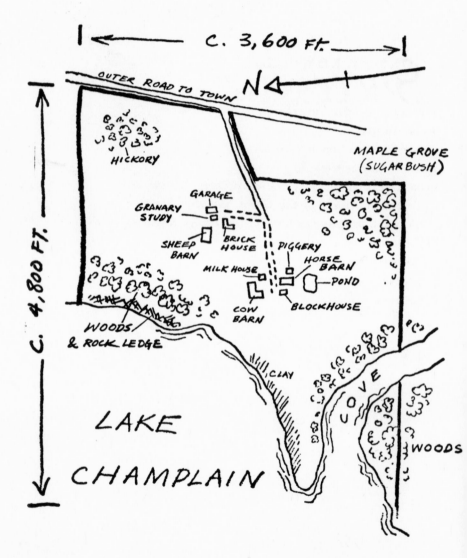

C. 3,600 FT.

N

OUTER ROAD TO TOWN

MAPLE GROVE
(SUGAR BUSH)

HICKORY

C. 4,800 FT.

GARAGE

GRANARY
STUDY

BRICK
HOUSE

SHEEP
BARN

PIGGERY

MILK HOUSE

HORSE
BARN

POND

COW
BARN

BLOCKHOUSE

WOODS
& ROCK LEDGE

CLAY

COVE

WOODS

LAKE

CHAMPLAIN

Successful
Calamity

A WRITER'S FOLLIES
ON A VERMONT FARM

BY *Edmund Fuller*

RANDOM HOUSE   *New York*

I wish to thank Mr. William L. Savage and other members of the Hand
family for permission to quote a letter from Judge Augustus N. Hand,
together with scattered passages from *The Letters of the Hand Family*,
edited by Susan Hand (Mrs. Augustus N. Hand).

To my Family,

who lived the adventure

Contents

Successful Calamity

CHAPTER ONE

Of Fits and Starts

THE WHOLE MAD ENTERPRISE of the farm began with a convulsion. It happened in the dead vast and middle of the night when I was awakened from sleep with the sudden, terrible belief that I was dying. I was shuddering all over—not merely quivering but thrashing—with a feeling of strangulation and an absolute conviction that I was shaking to pieces like a heavy engine with a shattered flywheel.

Insofar as I could think I supposed it to be some kind of heart attack, or else an epileptic fit. My wife, Ann, also was awakened by my noises of thrashing and gurgling, and jumped to the same horrified conclusion. The spasm went on for several minutes and then gradually abated, leaving both of us badly frightened and myself totally limp.

In the morning I hurried to the doctor, who checked me over in all the standard ways and then said, "I want you to see a neurologist. I'm sending you to Foster Kennedy."

"What could it be?" I pressed him.

"Well, for example . . . a brain tumor. He's the man who'll be able to tell you."

Foster Kennedy—since dead, alas, whereas here am I—was rated the leading neurologist by some doctors and ranked among the foremost by any. What interested me particularly was his collateral accomplishments which my doctor pointed out to me. He was literary and broadly interested in the arts, a physician who wrote articles not only for medical journals but also for *Saturday Review*. He involved himself in liberal causes and mingled with a miscellany of the great and the merely celebrated, from FDR to Harpo Marx. When I penetrated at last to his inner office, the walls made me feel as if I had blundered into Sardi's or some other place frequented by people who like to be near the pictures of the famous if they can't be near the famous themselves. In addition to the theatrical mob, which was well represented, the doctor's gallery ranged from Presidents of the United States and high military brass through a spectrum of authors and musicians, with a collection of framed letters, beginning "Dear Foster," to accompany the signed photos.

Dr. Kennedy himself was a short, heavy-set man who might have made a good wrestler if he'd had the dedication. He had a large, graying, balding head and a granitic cast of features that made him seem cousin to a Roman emperor. In his distinguished hands it seemed an honor to be sick. He looked over my own doctor's report of my clonic seizure, asked me some general questions, and gave me into the custody of an acolyte. This young man explored me from head to toe, probed, measured, X-rayed, and otherwise tested me. He studied the contours of several lumps on my skull, including one on the top of my head which seemed highly suspicious except for the fact that it had been there all my life, a stumbling block to unwary barbers, a lovely bump like the projecting small end of an egg mysteriously buried in my skull. It was a phrenologist's delight; I only hoped it would not prove a neurologist's nightmare.

I came back a few days later for the moment of truth with Dr. Kennedy. After some perfunctory checkup motions, like the final snips a barber administers, he gazed at me solemnly and said, "Fuller, your engine is too big for your chassis."

That admirable lead gave me at once the curious mixture of relief and disappointment which accompanies assurances that the loathsome disease has not got you, after all. Your flesh feels a reprieve but your ego feels an anticlimax. It's analogous to the vague feeling I have, when flying heavily insured, of being somehow the loser when we touch down safely.

Dr. Kennedy proceeded with a thumbnail sketch of my nervous system, to the conclusion that my spasm, convulsion, or fit was a delayed reaction of a frayed nervous structure to a more than ordinarily massive dose of novocaine I had been given during a nasty extraction some forty-eight hours preceding the attack. My own doctor had cited that as a possibility but had insisted quite properly that in the presence of symptoms, including the jumps and the bumps, which could mean more ominous things, he wanted it all checked out by a specialist.

The mana of impending dramatic disaster had departed from me and I was one more man listening to a reassuring and expensive anticlimax. Yet don't think me ungrateful.

Foster Kennedy proceeded to one of those sweeping recommendations that fall as lightly from the lips of doctors as their diatribes against socialized medicine, about changing one's entire way of life. I will say this was a thought far from repulsive, which had occurred to me already. Get out of offices, get out of the city; above all—be calm, calm, calm.

I sang the sad little song about pressure and necessity; we talked of the strains of office life, the city at large, and the peculiar, as yet barely realized, new strains of the postwar world that had got rid of Hitler, all right, but was still stuck with Stalin and the atom bomb.

Dr. Kennedy, like myself, was among those early exercised over the prospects the nuclear age held in store. In less than five minutes of his lecture on how I must de-pressurize my life, he was pounding on his desk with the flat of his hand and roaring at me in high Johnsonian style, "Fuller! You and I cannot *afford* to be calm!"

There was nothing left to do but pay the bill.

All the same, impetus and authority had been given to an already latent idea.

Just exactly what made us abandon everything and go to Vermont is not easy to sum up. It was a combination of romantic idealism and Foster Kennedy's imperative. There is the stark fact that a man can work up a good ulcer even when he loves what he is doing, if he is doing it under tension. I loved the book trade well enough, but unhappily I did, and even now still do, *everything* under tension—including relaxing. I unlimber in knots. I would go to lunch day after day with office colleagues, authors, or agents—talk, make plans, laugh, eat, achieve a lot, and enjoy it all thoroughly. Then, back in my office for a busy afternoon, I would feel rotating knives in my stomach.

Also, Ann and I were tired of being anchored to the city on a commuter's tether. Already we had given up city living for the suburbs for the sake of our children and ourselves. Now we were about to give up the suburbs for the frontier.

Our bucolic idealism was blended with my desire to try to go it alone as a free-lance writer, plus an urge toward true country living. That was what oriented us toward a farm.

So far as the publishing business was concerned, I had enjoyed it for eight years. An editor's life is one of those happy pursuits which seem inherently worth the effort, while at the same time, even in the best of publishing houses, there is enough sheer guff and mere merchandising involved to keep one from being either too arty or too pious. But at this time my interest was in leaving the desk, leaving the city, and finding a voice of my own. At hazard and with some trepidation I was out for the adventure of independence. Ann loyally professed to be in full accord, and I think partially was, though in the end it was to cost her more than it cost me.

When it was told in Gath and published in the streets of Ashkelon what we proposed to do, the news caused astonishment and some degree of consternation among our friends. One of them, the astute journalist George Britt, took me to lunch at the Players Club, and sitting across from me, in the best traditions of the setting, recited the long third-act speech from *Troilus and Cressida* in which Ulysses chides and admonishes the sulking Achilles, warning that if he hides himself in obscurity in his tent, the palm of fame will begin to pass, concluding:

> ". . . to have done, is to hang
> Quite out of fashion, like a rusty mail
> In monumental mockery . . .
> . . . The cry went once on thee,
> And still it might, and yet it may again,

If thou wouldst not entomb thyself alive,
And case thy reputation in thy tent . . ."

It was a context I found hard to fit, as I was not a man on whom the cry had ever greatly gone. When he saw that I was not to be deterred George shook his head sorrowfully and said, "Edmund, I simply cannot understand how a man can deliberately change everything else in his life and not change his wife, too."

What was there to say? A man must have some continuity; and George didn't know my wife.

Thus from a fit there came a start.

CHAPTER TWO

264 Acres of Snow

. I FEEL SURE that we are the only people who ever set forth in January and bought a Vermont farm under four feet of snow. For all we could tell, other than by test borings, we might have been buying 264 acres paved with cement. For us it was the reverse of the old romantic-song cliché. Our concern about the farm was: Will we love you in June as we love you in January?

The whole thing was done backward. We didn't have a farm at the time we reached our decision and made our vital commitments. We just knew that we wanted one—were determined to have one. When I had announced the word and resigned from my job it then became a matter of finding ourselves a farm to which to go.

If I ever knew why we did that in January, I don't any longer. It is a matter of record that we did. It simply *was* January—and what a January! The whole holiday season had been building up to it. The day before Christmas in '47 brought an epic snowstorm of twenty-six inches. Everything was beautiful, with an ice storm to glaze the drifts. The lights were off for a whole day. The New Year piled another ice-and-sleet storm on top of that. Still more snow came on the sixth of January and again on the thirteenth.

We had made plans to start for Vermont on Thursday, January 15, 1948, and had lined up in advance, through personal contacts and correspondence with real estate agents, a number of farm properties from southern to northern Vermont which we were going to inspect.

Before proceeding further, we had better check the cast of characters. Who were we? There were Ann and myself; then Graham, our oldest boy, ten; David, six; and our daughter Meredith, who was only two. Also, there was an added starter. Ann and I had begun planning the move solely on our own. When her mother, Virginia Graham, who lived near us in Nyack, heard the news of the enterprise she announced that she was going to sell out and come along, too, jointly or separately. So we decided that if we were all leaving, we might as well pool our resources and operate together.

Thus, on our wintry reconnaissance trip there were Ann and myself, Graham and David, and Virginia. Meredith was left behind in safe keeping. Ann did the driving. It was an art, by the way, which I had not yet mastered at my then thirty-four years but which I was to acquire quickly in Vermont. It seems, in fact, that there are a great many talents that I have developed in middle life, including driving, swimming, milking, tennis playing, and, for that matter, considerably later, drinking. For all its vicissitudes, the farm was not responsible for the last.

We started for Vermont at nine in the morning, in the worst winter conditions the Hudson Valley had seen in years.

All the way from Nyack to West Point, along Old Route 9-W, road conditions were so wretched and hazardous and progress so slow that we began to despair of reaching Vermont that day. But beyond West Point the skies cleared and we were moving constantly toward regions better prepared to cope with snow, so that the roads gradually improved.

Spirits were high with the collective family sense that we were undertaking something that no family in its right mind would attempt, which carried a certain exhilaration with it. David was in fine form with his rare capacity for a kind of ruminative irrelevance. He would be silent for long stretches of time and then suddenly come up with an observation or question with absolutely no external context or forewarning, but stemming wholly from his own unfathomable reverie.

As we whipped through the white and high-drifted countryside he asked abruptly, "Mommy, would ten cabbages weigh more than a cat?"

Ann was the recipient of many of his memorable utterances, and one of the richest times for them, just as there are advantageous times of the day for fishing, was lunch, which she generally had alone with him while Graham was in school. Once he rejected his milk and when asked why, said, "It tastes like owl's blood." The flavor has become a tradition in our family.

It was also David who created the splendid word "pestimist" as antonym of "optimist."

We arrived in Bennington, Vermont, by dark. It was bitter cold, working down toward the deep sub-zeros of the night before. We stayed at the old Hotel Putnam, which was bitterly hot in the way of old-fashioned steam-heated hotels. David milled around the lobby with Graham, both engagingly communicative, passing the word to all who would hear and the few who could believe, how we had come north to acquire a farm.

David was a tow-headed radiator of good will. He came into the world exuding amiability. We have photographs of David and Graham, each at thirteen months old. They're a comic contrast, not wholly by chance but with some true capturing of personality. In these portraits David has an immense cherubic smile that also gleams in the eyes looking inward upon bliss. He is surely saying, "Hence, loathéd Melancholy . . ." Graham's visage is a study in infant *Angst*, unmistakably crying, "Hence, vain deluding Joys . . ." Ann and I have known this pair of pictures always as "L'Allegro" and "Il Penseroso."

This original beamish boy, David, excused himself during dinner at the Hotel Putnam to go to the bathroom. I gave him the old-fashioned kitchen-door type of key to our room and he departed. Engrossed in our own conversations, we were unmindful of his absence until my gaze fell on his chair and I realized he had been gone from the table for some time. We worried that he might have an upset stomach or some swift-striking flu germ. I went out to the desk in the lobby and asked the switchboard to ring our room. There was no answer to the repeated rings. I thought he was bound to the bathroom by dire necessity and hastened up to the third floor.

The door to the room was locked. I rapped on it and rattled the handle, calling out, "David! David! Are you in there? Are you all right?" No answer. I stooped to the keyhole—there was no key in it from the inside. I hurried back down to the dining room—still no David there.

Perplexed more than alarmed—it seemed neither the country nor season for kidnapers—we got up from our unfinished dinner, leaving only Ann's mother in case David returned, and deployed through the hotel. The desk, too, was alerted, ready to start a phone poll of rooms if need be. It was a small old hotel with rambling corridors. Graham, Ann, and I patrolled the floors, quietly calling out David's name from time to time—not yet wishing to bellow a general alarm.

We converged again upon the lobby. Interested spectators were offering theories, Virginia was peering out of the dining room, someone speculated about the cellar, and real worry was just assailing us when David came down the stairs, beaming, hand in hand with a white-haired woman who was a resident of the hotel. Vaguely I remembered that she had been in the dining room before David left.

We pounced. "Where in the world have you been?"

His friend said, "Well, I'm afraid I've kept him too long. He's such an interesting little boy."

"But how on earth . . . ?"

"I went to the bathroom in her room," David said. "I got mixed up about the floor, and the door wasn't locked . . ."

"I'm on the floor below you," the woman said. "When I came up from dinner I heard someone humming in my bathroom, and there he was."

"She was surprised," David said. He seemed not to have been.

"Yes, I was. But then we had a lovely visit and I've heard all about your trip. I think you're all very brave people."

We exchanged pleasantries and hastened back to resume our gelid meal.

"I should think *you* were the one surprised," Graham said.

"Yes," David said, showing clearly that serenity had never fled him, "except I thought it was funny that I didn't see the suitcases . . . My meat is cold."

On Friday morning, the sixteenth, it was snowing hard.

Nevertheless we followed an agent over slippery roads to adjacent White Creek, New York. We got stuck and were pulled out by a farm truck. The place we inspected had nice buildings, good location, but no woods and no body of water —features on at least one of which our hopeful hearts were set.

We went back to Bennington, picked up our bags, and pushed north toward Middlebury, the snow stopping a little past midday. In Manchester, we paused to introduce ourselves to Walter Hard and his wife, proprietors of the Johnny Appleseed Bookshop. Strangers though we were, they received us with characteristic instant hospitality and encouraged our madness. We were to come to know them well and affectionately. Walter was a regional poet, one of three or four writers who have most captured the savor and quality of his state in such books as A *Mountain Township* and A *Matter of Fifty Houses*. To Walter and Marjorie Hard it was purely natural and rational that anyone should come to Vermont to stay, irrespective of season or weather.

It was dark when we got to Middlebury and stopped at the Inn there. We kept the flock close so there would be no straying through wrong corridors and bathrooms. Saturday morning it was snowing hard again. Undaunted, we let the most lugubrious real estate agent I have ever seen drive us in his own car to a town and a farm over on Lake Champlain. The farm was not inhabited at the time and we found that the half-mile entrance road was not plowed out.

Ann, the boys, and I set out from the mailbox and floundered and bucked our way through alternating level snow and dune-like drifts toward the house. It was strenuous, slow, and fun.

Opposite the entrance was a modest farmhouse where Virginia found a French-Canadian farmer who obligingly hitched up a team to a massive flat sled that may also have been what is called a stone boat. Virginia and the agent clambered aboard with the farmer, who broke through with the team on our trail and delivered Virginia at the main house.

It was a good-looking brick building on an elevation with fine trees around it, sloping down to a great expanse of frozen and snow-covered lake. In the background, westward across the lake, rose several ranges of Adirondacks, of which then we could see only the first tier dimly, as it was still snowing. Near the brick house were a garage, a sheep barn, and other outbuildings in various states of repair, and farther down the road toward the lake was a smaller frame house, also with barns around it.

We were impressed. The French Canadian, presumably with no ax to grind, had worked part of the land for the owner and gave good report of it. The asking price was substantially more than we had hoped to pay.

Going back to the outer road, all of us accepted a lift on the great flat sled. It was fun of a rigorous sort, relished especially by the boys: the gliding motion, the snorting, laboring team with jingling harness bells, biting wind, snow blowing in our faces, the ghostly white but splendid landscape.

That same afternoon we left Middlebury and, though the snow never abated, pushed farther north, reaching Burlington in the dusk. We stopped at the old and seedy Van Ness House. It has since burned down, probably to few people's regret—certainly not to mine—and it was so hot that night that I thought it was burning down already.

Sunday morning was very cold and at last clear. We drove some forty miles easterly into the highest of the Green Mountains, lovely and alarming, to a place called Johnson.

There we saw a beautiful farm, almost Alpine, wild and woodsy, with a huge sugarbush and a professional sugar house. The boys went sledding on the farmer's hills. We sank into drifts with the car and our host dragged us out with his tractor. We were much taken by the farm and its cordial owner, but were firmly convinced, as he was too, that it would be hopelessly beyond our abilities to manage. He would not have wished to sell to us if we had wished to buy.

When we got back to Burlington by night the temperature was sinking rapidly toward twenty below. Monday morning, the nineteenth, we journeyed at eight below zero to Malletts Bay and looked quickly at a farm too small and run down.

It had come to seem to all of us that the lake farm was the best prospect. We headed briskly for Middlebury to inspect it further and bargain with the owner. Meanwhile the now hopeful agent, perceiving with his own eyes the follies of which we were capable, had had the road to the two houses plowed out, though not so thoroughly that we didn't have minor difficulties.

The details of the place were richly appealing to us, especially, as you would suppose, those aspects that would be of no interest to the practical farmer but were naturals for mad folk of our kind.

The authentic history of the farm was a dream equally for a romanticist or a historian—which is not to suggest that the two are mutually exclusive. We are people with singular responsiveness to aura, and in addition to its beauty of location this farm was freighted with aura.

It was called Hand's Cove, an old seat of the family from which sprang the two distinguished United States Circuit Court judges—first cousins and among the great jurists of their age—Augustus and Learned Hand. Both had spent much of their boyhood there.

The old tenant house—called the blockhouse for reasons which we will take up later—was built around 1763 by one Samuel Herrick, first owner of the land, and acquired about 1792 by Nathan Hand. The brick house was built in 1840, on the commanding rise. The blockhouse lay some quarter of a mile and at a lower level southwest of it. From that, in turn, the fields and pastures swept down and away toward a great promontory of land jutting far into Lake Champlain.

Ticonderoga, New York, was on the opposite side, and in all but the winter months, a rude ferry plied back and forth from a point just south of the farm. From the lawn of the brick house we had a splendid view of old Fort Ticonderoga across the lake against the bastion of Mount Defiance. Its flag flying, the fort was a sight stark and picturesquely brooding at any time, but especially imposing in the winter scene.

The promontory mentioned above formed the north side of a deep wooded cove, from which the farm took its name, and in which Ethan Allen, in 1776, marshaled his assortment of barges and rowboats and sallied across the lake by night for the surprise and capture of Ticonderoga. There, at the time of the enterprise, he had a rendezvous with Benedict Arnold, then still a hero of the Revolutionary cause, who was on this occasion vexed that the leadership of this sortie was firmly in the hands of this local, wild Green Mountain Boy.

Members of the Hand family held the property from 1792 until about 1945. The last purchaser died shortly after the transaction, and his widow, having occupied it very little, was eager to get it off her hands.

As we prowled around on this second visit, along with aura we also found omens. There were several large bookcases in the hallway of the brick house, full of old books abandoned by the last of the resident Hand family. Scanning these, as I do compulsively with any shelves of books of any vintage anywhere, I came across two large leather-bound volumes, gold-stamped on their spines: *Fuller's Works*. These were part of the writings of the seventeenth-century English divine and historian, the Rev. Thomas Fuller, author of, among other things, *The Worthies of England*. For me, in that time and place, it was an omen not to be resisted. We no longer have the farm, but I still have the two volumes of Fuller's works, plus several that the present Fuller accomplished there, not without difficulty but not without pride.

We hastened back to Middlebury for a late afternoon conference with the owner in the lobby of the Inn. We asked questions, garnered information about the standing arrangements that she had made with neighboring farmers for the cutting and sharing of the hay crops, and much else. We bargained, excused ourselves from time to time for excited and tense consultations in our own rooms. Should we? Shouldn't we? Everything about the place seemed just right for us. The move was ambitious; it was precipitate. Well, we had known all that; if we had meant to think in cautious terms we need not have come incontinently to Vermont in the chill middle of the winter, and I might as well not have announced an irrevocable resignation from a good job.

For better or worse—and it has been some of each—we have never been hesitaters. We act, once we have committed ourselves, and act quickly. We had a vision of how we would develop this place for both Ann's and my purposes and Virginia's. We reached a compromise price, and then and there, in the lobby of the Middlebury Inn, on Monday afternoon, January 19, 1948, we signed a contract of sale and made a down payment on the Hand's Cove farm. The 264 acres comprised nearly two miles of in-and-out lake frontage, including both sides of the historic cove, some one hundred acres of pasture, some seventy-five to a hundred in woods, and the rest in good meadow. We had our water and our woods.

Some of our city friends, when the news was issued, were uncertain about the nice distinction between pasture and meadow. Pasture, of course, is grazing land; meadow is a mead for mowing, the place where the hay crop is raised. Thus in the nursery rhyme about the intransigent little boy blue: "The sheep's in the meadow, the cow's in the corn," where neither of them ought to be, both belonging in pastures.

A closing date was set for April 1, and to my pleasure the owner threw in a privately printed volume, *The Letters of the Hand Family*, compiled by the wife of Judge Augustus Hand, containing the history of the property, and also Pell's life of Ethan Allen, with particulars about the action in the cove.

All of us were in high and hectic spirits, the boys immensely excited. Ann and I, in truth, felt overwhelmed. When the dust had settled we went out by ourselves into the cold evening for a walk in the snow-piled streets of Middlebury. At that moment, in the exhilaration of decision and action, we had scant misgivings left. We have always been adventuresome, willing to risk things on ourselves, to gamble on our own performance. Above all, it has been a mutual confidence that we could work things out, for all our known frailty and variability in the human lot. We walked arm in arm, briskly, around the town square, breathing forth dragon-clouds of steam, nostril hairs prickling with the fierce, dry cold. And we laughed.

Afterward we stopped in the old diner on the square for coffee and pie. The place was rebuilt and modernized a few years later, but we always remember it as then. The counter man, a burly but gentle-spirited fellow, put my coffee down directly on the counter in a thick white mug. Ann's came in an equally thick cup of bounceable crockery, but with a saucer. I asked, "How come I don't get a saucer?" The counter man looked embarrassed, ducked his head, and said, "Well . . . for the lady it's more daintier."

The owner had turned over to us a huge surveyor's map of the property, on brown paper. The next morning I took it to a photographer and had it reproduced in five by seven for practical reference. Then Ann and I did what more conventionally would have been done before the closing of the deal —but this was our backward way. We visited the Middlebury office of the U.S. Soil Conservation Service and saw the agent, whose own home was near our farm. He was infinitely patient and helpful, as were all the federal, state, and county farm and forest agencies that we were to deal with in the next few years.

We hadn't seen a trace of the considerable expanse of soil that we had purchased—only its four feet of white icing, and its trees. Even the existence of Lake Champlain was taken on faith and report, for it manifested itself to our eyes only as so much additional snow-covered pasture.

The map had revealed the shape of the farm to be extraordinarily like a miniature Texas, which reminded me of the traditional Vermont boast that if the state were ironed out flat it would be bigger than Texas. Actually the great promontory thrust out into the lake much in the shape of a cow's teat, which was again an omen.

As for the nature of what lay beneath the snow on all this acreage, the Soil Conservation office had genuine treasures for us, which we greeted with delight and carried away for hours of close study. There were aerial photographs of the entire farm, many sections of it in detail, augmented by carefully plotted ground plans, marked out in varicolored crayons, representing analyses of the kind of soil in each sector, with recommendations for its best use or treatment.

Armed with our documents and trophies, we headed south, mission triumphantly accomplished. Lodging again at the Putnam, in Bennington, we found that its manager had been a former neighbor of the Hand's Cove farm. He contributed lore about it, all happily encouraging, while David, cruising the lobby as before, told all and sundry astonished listeners about our prize.

Next morning, Wednesday, it was snowing heavily once more. We had a plodding, bad day's drive, worst of all on the home stretch, just as it had been when we set out. We made it by about seven o'clock, tired and happy, with a buried undercurrent of bewilderment and consternation. We had our farm—or it had us.

CHAPTER THREE

The Farm Family Fuller

I CONVEYED MY NEWS elatedly to the office next morning.
It aroused seething excitement from all hands. There followed days, weeks, indeed a total season of incredible correspondence and consultation, with lawyers, bankers, government agencies. Miscellaneous information was offered by everybody from old friends to new acquaintances, covering all
subjects from how to scale logs to estimate their potential
board footage of lumber, to plumbing, the merits of pumps,
electric or gasoline; home generators; sugar making, and
beekeeping—this from our lawyer, Bernard Grossman, who
once kept hives in New York City and had written a book on
bees.

Our literature included an enthralling pamphlet from
Cornell University on "Wild Foods." Its range was astonishing but it was disquieting because of the constant exhortation
to caution about a vast number of poisonous, or simply loath-

some, plants, a few of which were edible if treated just so. Its delights included stinging nettle ("Boiling removes sting. Wear gloves when gathering . . .") and amaranth pigweed.

For skunk cabbage (*Symplocarpus foetidus*), abundant in the cove, one was instructed to "Cook tender, discarding one or two waters. Cooking reduces offensiveness. . . . Emergency food only. . . ." The green arrow arum is "acrid and poisonous when fresh, eaten safely after long roasting or boiling. . . ."

There were numerous wild "teas" and coffee substitutes. Recipes were offered for such delicacies as buttered nettles, cattail-pollen pancakes, elderflower waffles, and sumac "lemonade."

For meat, one might choose among fricasseed muskrat, roast woodchuck, and porcupine liver with bacon. Also crow, for those whom circumstances required to eat it.

We read all of this with fascination but took none of it beyond the hypothetical stage. Still, I found it comforting to feel that in abject poverty I would have more resources than simply grazing in my own green pastures like a latter-day Nebuchadnezzar.

Among the most touching phenomena were spontaneous offers of loans from friends who wouldn't have done more than dream of what we were doing but dearly loved to identify vicariously with the adventure. I availed myself of some of those offers before I was through on the farm.

A few weeks after the buying expedition, I took leave permanently of my office, with appropriate farewell winings and dinings. Among other gestures, I was presented with the desk and chair that I had used in my office for some years, and which, indeed, I have used not only at the farm but ever since, including this work in hand.

There lay ahead of me far more than I realized of literal fence mending. But now, as we began to organize ourselves for the move, with the harrowing details of selling our Nyack property and taking full title to the farm, I set about the metaphoric fence mending of all my contacts with publishing houses and literary agents, with whom I hoped to function as a free-lance editorial consultant. Also I established ties with book-review media. Through all these I hoped both to provide a sufficient income and keep my hand and name professionally active in the book trade.

The great move began on April 26. It took all day for movers and packers to load four vans with the contents of two houses, ours and Virginia's. Our van pulled away from the door around six o'clock in the evening. We were on the road by quarter to seven, by now almost too exhausted to feel the wrench of departure from a lovely house that had harbored happy years. We traveled just far enough for the gesture of starting, halting overnight in Newburgh.

The next day we reached the farm by four in the afternoon, ahead of the movers, which meant we had no place to lay our heads unless they arrived. Everything struck us as marvelously beautiful, beyond any vision or sight we had had of the place before. The white mantle of January had given way to the burgeoning spring green in trees and meadow. The waters of Lake Champlain rippled and gleamed, and the four distinct tiers of Adirondacks ranged westward and north from the lake. As we stood under the elms on the lawn of the brick house, looking down past the dirty white of the other dwelling which we called the blockhouse, we saw the glint of water in the historic, Allen-haunted cove.

We wandered through the empty houses and also took renewed inventory of the buildings. At the rear corner of the brick house was a two-car garage, and through a rear door of it, a small chicken house. Next to the garage, closer to the house, was a small two-story granary. This was to be remodeled and weather-tightened as an office for me. Behind the granary was an odd and unaccountable small single-roomed building, with a window and a finished hardwood floor. We decided to place our chemical toilet there until our plumbing was installed; after that it could be an outside guest room.

A small tool shed stood apart, behind the brick house. Then some five hundred feet west was the large sheep barn which, as we had learned from *The Letters of the Hand Family*, once had housed the proud, long-vanished Merino sheep, the livestock aristocrats of Vermont farming in the nineteenth century. In the ironies of agriculture, the overgrazing of such sheep contributed to the exhaustion of much Vermont soil, especially in the sparse hill towns.

The blockhouse, to the southwest, was the center of another cluster of buildings. Close beside it was a dilapidated horse barn. Beyond that was the skeleton of an icehouse, a mere frame of heavy, hand-hewn timber. Its floor was a vast depth of sawdust, which had once packed and insulated the ice blocks sawed from the winter lake and stored for summer use. Behind this wreck was a piggery in some disrepair.

Opposite the blockhouse were the large L-shaped cow barn and its enclosed yard. In the corner of the barnyard, at the terminus of the clay road, was the little milk house, which had no equipment in it but the sunken concrete tub in which milk cans had been cooled in water.

There was limited electric wiring in the brick house—none in any other building; no plumbing in either house except for old-fashioned hand pumps connected to rain-water cisterns, of which only the one in the brick house was operable at present. We knew the ensuing spring nights would be cold —and possibly some days. There was no heat in the house except what we could get up in the wood-and-coal-burning range already in the kitchen, and a portable kerosene heater that would arrive with the furniture.

We were marking time. With the excited boys—David wholly enthusiastic and even Graham captured in spite of some reluctance to leave familiar surroundings and friends— we wandered through the woods along the northern stretch of lakeshore to a two-room frame camp-style shack among the pine trees on a jut of land that thrust out over the water on a rocky overhang. Below it was a slaty beach, beyond which the woods stretched farther along rocky shore.

We felt a sense of endless treasure and discovery ahead of us. It was a reward for our boldness in buying the farm with such minimal acquaintance with it. There were to be penalties for such rashness in other ways, but that was yet to be revealed.

Back at the house we ate our picnic-style supper, having eaten a main meal at midday on the road. Dusk was falling and we despaired, in the gathering chill. We had just concluded we would have to go to Middlebury for the night when the boys set up a shout. Along the outer road, silhouetted against the darkling sky, our caravan was crawling. It hesitated, taking notice of our name fastened by makeshift to the mailbox, and turned in toward us. We learned later that the procession, stopping to ask directions in the village, had the whole community—including all the farms along the way— agog with curiosity at the arriving city people with four truckloads of lares and penates. Among the rumors, I learned later from our affable mailman, was one to the effect that I was a poet and made $10,000 a year. Well—the village was remote from the world of letters. How were they to know?

It was after seven o'clock. All that was feasible was to take off some beds prudently placed in the back of the smallest of the vans. Then the moving crew went off in it to find lodging. We all slept in our clothes under blankets on otherwise unmade beds, going to bed at once, for there was nothing else to do and no other way to keep warm, though we were burning wood in the kitchen range.

It was a restive, wakeful night for all of us, between the cold and the excitement. In the dark, no light in the house, I stepped outside to look upon the hedge, and caught my breath at the night sky in our glorious solitude and stillness. It was a brilliant vault of stars in the clear, cold blackness— the great western star miraculously large and bright to one too long in populous city pent. I was tired and, in fact, a little frightened at what we had begun, but the air was clear and we had a dream that impelled us on our way. Whatsoever we had been before, we were a new, strange entity now—we had become the farm family Fuller.

CHAPTER FOUR

Letters from an American Farmer

THERE WAS a euphoric headiness to that first spring and summer that even the harassments of adaptation and a few sharp shocks could not dampen. There was, too, a gamesomeness, a high-hearted will to adventure and risk in all of us. There were also elements of rashness, folly, and naïveté—clear in hindsight, though even then we knew they must be present. Yet I was—and still am—proud of each of us.

We had a master plan that imposed a logic upon our variegated assortment of buildings. Though Ann and I had the large family, we were going to live in the small house. Our income, presumably, was in my head. Hopefully, from my erstwhile-granary office were to flow works to establish an ever-normal granary for the Fuller family.

Virginia, who in her diversified career had run a variety of restaurants and guest houses, was to operate the brick house as an inn, with special attention to vacation bookings, of which I expected, rightly, to drum up a good many. Indeed, they began almost as fast as we unpacked.

The brick house had a frame wing which, besides the kitchen, held some small rooms that could be loosely considered as an apartment. Ann and I, with the children, were to occupy these rooms until the blockhouse could be made habitable.

The fury of activity in the ensuing weeks almost defies report. It is exhausting just to review the terse record in my compact but comprehensive diary. It includes banking and credit arrangements; consultations with two farmers about leasing of meadows, pastures, and sharing of hay crops; procuring of advice, estimates, and bids from electricians, plumbers, furnace men, and carpenters; putting in of kitchen gardens; planning for the acquisition of animals and chickens; building of a fireplace and chimney in the brick house; remodeling; water problems; correspondence; neighbors and other people to meet; doctors and dentists to locate; arrangements for Graham to begin school at once; fishing lore to learn; a boat to buy; professional work of my own to keep up. Little of this was a once-for-all proposition; most was a continuing process that stretched from weeks to months. It all ran together frenziedly. To recollect it in tranquillity requires isolating for examination one part at a time of what, in reality, happened simultaneously.

The helter-skelter, the dazzling tumble of events, and also the vital élan of the early weeks were captured partly in a spate of letters that I wrote, though where I got the energy or time to write them, on top of this vast upheaval of our way of life, mystifies me still.

An engaging Frenchman, one-time consul in Colonial New York and temporary settler in the upper reaches of that state, was St. John de Crèvecoeur, author of *Letters from an American Farmer*. He was a friend of Ethan Allen, who named St. Johnsbury, Vermont, in his honor. This chapter is a doff of my hat to Crèvecoeur.

Samplings of my own latter-day letters from an American farmer, written to diverse persons, fill, as nothing else can, the gaps between the larger set pieces of our experience, capturing its immediacy. Not the least poignant aspect of these records is the eagerly projected plans that never came to fulfillment. The letters from which these passages are culled were written to my mother; my father's brothers, who had all grown up on an Iowa farm; my three sisters, especially Annette who was dying of cancer; and to friends and colleagues from the office and elsewhere. The letters have not been doctored but are as written, with an occasional comment in brackets.

May 4

. . . the moving went off quite smoothly and the weather was wonderful. It is now and has been except for three days of intermittent cold rain. In coming here we turned the calendar back just about exactly three weeks as compared to Nyack . . . The apple orchards are in bud but even the cherries are not in bloom yet.

We've lived a little primitively for a few days, improvising heat with our old portable oil stove, plus the kitchen range and the oven of the electric stove. We're under control now and our quarters are nice and comfortable. It is good and warm in the sun and warming continually.

Such a hum of activity! There are carpenters doing work here now. Men scurry in and out making surveys and estimates on heating systems and the water system. Plans seem to be coming along smoothly in these directions, with no snags yet visible and some things looking better than we had anticipated so far as the problems go.

[Fatuous illusion!]

Oh, yes. Our neighbors. Everyone has been wonderful. The whole town was agog as our vans rolled through and all along the dirt roads back to the farm. Mrs. Stalker brought us a beautiful cake. A day or so later Mrs. Heitman brought us a cherry pie. Various others have called and expressed the desire to be helpful in any way. People are extremely pleasant.

It is such a pleasure to see farmer D——'s herd grazing in our pasture. They roam all around and one encounters them at times among the trees or you see them down on the big point, far out into the lake. They are young cattle and mistrustful of strangers and go trotting off elsewhere whenever we cross the pasture near them.

Then our fields are humming. Both D—— and B——, who are sharing the farm this summer, are plowing. Tractors buzz in and out. And yesterday D—— put in his oats, at the same time putting in alfalfa, red clover, and timothy for us. These operations tell us more about the farm than anything else. It is beautiful, rich land.

From B—— we buy our milk, now. Five quarts a day of whole milk always from the same cow. We pay 15¢ a quart and from this we take our butterfat from which we shall make butter, and also we get our cream for general use . . .

I can scarcely speak of the view adequately. Not only the lake and the great ranges of mountains, but we look from high ground down across woods and orchards and coves. Our woods are nice. And I have enough hickory groves to start a nut industry.

The boys are fine and enjoying themselves hugely. Graham has just begun school and is griping a little. Virginia is working furiously and we have had a great putting in of plants and trees that we had lugged up with us. We keep farm hours, pretty much.

Oh, I forgot the helicopter! We had a great show on Saturday or Friday, I guess. Near here is the orchard of an awfully nice man named Witherell. His boy Sandy is already a good friend of Graham's. Well, a Bell helicopter flew over, low, one day, to our astonishment. Then we were driving into the village and saw it in Witherell's meadow. So we got out and joined the crowd. Turned out it was from the University at Burlington, giving a demonstration of dusting orchards by helicopter, which seems to be quite a thing. So we watched, standing right in the rotor wash, while it went through all its paces like a huge, plastic bumblebee . . .

It is not all beer and skittles and a vast idyll. We are working plenty hard and have lots of things to solve and work out. But we are full of confidence and determination and these nice things are the things that make it worth doing. Nothing has gone wrong yet, but it is certain sure that some things will and when they do we expect to take the bad with the good with the best good will and resourcefulness we can muster.

May 20

One of the largest items, possibly not included before, is the butter making. Ann now makes it regularly and it is fascinating and delicious. Our churn, which a relative of Ann's has promised us, has not yet arrived and she does it all with the electric mixer. The heavy cream from the whole milk— the butterfat, rather—first makes a heavy whipped cream, then it begins to thin out to a watery total loss, then all of a sudden, hard yellow globules start forming until they become thick in the thin skim milk and are gathered and pressed together into a big lump of butter. Its color looks almost artificial, for the milk is very rich . . .

When it's windy up here, by the way, it's a powerful wind. It roars down the slopes of the Adirondacks and across the lake with a whoop-de-do that is something to hear. Wait'll it roars around here in winter . . .

[Oh, my prophetic soul!]

. . . But if all our neighbors thrive in it, we can.

The orchards are just beginning to open into bloom, which will give some idea of our timetable.

Furious work still goes on on all sides. A fireplace and a chimney for the furnace, all in one, are going up on the brick house. The sealed up fireplaces in the frame house have now been opened and are quite something, some of them with the old kettle cranes still in them. Electricians, carpenters, masons and plumbers are all working at once. Everything is within our plans and calculations, but of course it is momentarily appalling, now and then, to behold the scope and actuality of this vast program to which one is committed. David is having the time of his life, for he hangs on all this avidly. Yesterday a huge pit was dug for the septic tank and trenches for pipe are spreading around. There's quite a story with the well, much too big to start on now.

Tomorrow I shall move out of the room in which I have had my temporary office, for it is to become the bathroom. Even though it is not all finished off, I shall move into my new, permanent office. This is in the old granary, a nice small building maybe something like thirty by twenty feet, with two stories. The old grain bins have been taken out. My desk and files and such will be on the second floor, separated only by a short, open stair from the ground floor. It is all being insulated and sealed and finished off with insulite boarding, laid in between the big old beams so that it has a timbered effect. It has been wired and I shall have myself quite a place, separated from the activities in and around the house. I will have a stove in it for winter.

As exciting an experience as we have had was the visit last week of the County Farm Agent of the U.S. Soil Conservation Office and the County Forester. They are grand people. Ann and I spent hours with them, going over the whole farm (which is an exhausting trip, by the way). We have worked out a three-point program for its long range development. Plantings, next spring, of thousands (that's right) of shrubs and trees along the north side of the big point where the lake is eating into the soil in terms of rods each year. This goes on all along the lake except on the wooded and rocky portions of the shoreline. The government provides all the trees and shrubs and will go to any length to arrest this process everywhere.

Second and easiest, a portion of our biggest pasture area will get a thorough lime and super-phosphate application to restore to lush grass what is now thinning out. This thinning has just begun and they say one season will restore it.

Third, the forester says we have the best maple grove (sugarbush, they call it, too) that he has seen along the lake. But in it, and other portions of our woods, cattle have been allowed to graze for years. He showed us wherein we would have had a splendid new growth of maple if it hadn't been grazed off every year. We are at once fencing the cattle out of all woods, maple and otherwise. I shall do the fencing myself . . . We shall begin at once and cover the most important areas first. Also we shall fence the cattle away from the eroding lakeshore, which they do not help any.

Mayville, the Farm Agent, is mapping the best fence courses for me to solve these problems and not limit the cattle from all the grazing and water they need. Our long-range idea, in the back of our minds, which he endorses as ideal for this farm, is a grass farm for some beef cattle of our own, a few years from now. This is all future, of course, but it represents a direction, which we must have in our minds if we are to do anything.

Well, there is more to tell but no more time to tell it in. Communiqué number three will follow at some indefinite time. We are all wonderfully well, laboring mightily, and eating heavily. It certainly is the complete readjustment of living that I expected, but I can scarcely remember anything that went before it, just now.

May 22 [to a former office colleague]

You said in one of your previous letters that things must seem quite "remote" to me. Yes, they do, in a way that I have not experienced before. I am caught up in the requirements and absorptions of a new way, with lots of experience and much necessary work. News seems at a distance and many things that used to be in the forefront of my consciousness—magazines and things like that—seem not to exist.

[We received New York papers by mail, one day late, which we found lent a refreshing perspective and decompression to news.]

If I were given the assignment, I could write an ingenious piece showing how "bad" that is from a lot of angles. But I do not think it is bad at all. I have been too much in the world, and too much in various patterns of action for "isolation." What I hope to gain is some judgment, an opportunity for appraisal, and the chance to use the knowledge and observation that I have acquired to the best purposes to which my ability will enable me to put them. Also I am testing certain old values and acquiring certain new ones.

[My father and his three brothers had grown up on a working farm in Iowa. When I was a child my father told me tales of his boyhood there. Alas, he had died nearly ten years before we brought our farm, but I wrote a joint letter to my three uncles outlining the whole venture. What stands out in it is my attempt to explain what motivated us.]

May 23

. . . The reasons behind this are numerous. For one thing we have no faith in cities or the ways of cities or any area within the influence of cities. We have no faith in dependence upon systems of service and supply. We have seen them fail or falter around us often in the last few years and we have seen the paralysis and helplessness that can result. Come another war, we know what this will mean, though we are in no sense moving because of anticipation of war. But we do want to learn something about a saner way of life and a more resourceful, more self-sufficient way.

For my part, though I have had some success in it, I abhor the so-called literary circle in the city. I have always avoided it and hurried home to do my own work out of hours. But a taxing, full-time desk job, both creative and administrative, and the nighttime effort in which I have produced several books have been more than I can stand any longer. I have two book commitments which I do not believe I could carry out the same old way . . . I am, on the other hand, eager to test my own capacities for creative work to the utmost . . .

We have begun openly to all on the premise that we know nothing whatever about farming but are out with all our might and main to learn from the ground up . . .

We are launched under favorable and promising circumstances. We know many things can and will go wrong and are braced for it. It must work for we have sunk our grub-stake in it and it has got to work. It is not the free-flowing-cash, retired-man kind of proposition. (I should hope not, at thirty-four!) But between my professional work and the attempt to manage the farm intelligently it will work out or be our own fault.

It is a terrible regret to me that Papa is not living to see this place. He would have been crazy about it and I think he would have been fascinated, if nothing else, at this venture (possibly even horrified, but I think not). But how he would have liked this farm! It would have warmed his heart.

June 12 [another phase of Vermont experience]

Wednesday, upon invitation, we all drove eighty miles down to Arlington and had a nice visit with Dorothy Canfield Fisher, who was most cordial and gracious. We also visited an architect and author of books on Vermont covered bridges and houses, Herbert Wheaton Congdon, who lives nearby. Mrs. Fisher taught us a lesson in reforestation, taking us through a beautiful tract of white pine which she and her husband planted themselves about thirty-seven years ago. Its carpet of needles was rich in pink lady-slippers. Graham had a

[37]

nice experience. He and David disappeared in the woods and returned after a time reporting the discovery of some awfully nice people who had fed them cookies and whom they insisted we come up to see. We did, later. They lived in a house up in Mrs. Fisher's woods and she told us they were a Professor Baumgardt and wife. He was the leading philosopher of the University of Berlin until he fled from Hitler. He is now with the Library of Congress as a consultant but spends his summers here working on the tomes he writes for the university press field. Well, anyway, he was a nice man with a rich accent, and he and Graham were mutually entranced. They talked astronomy and Graham told him about seeing *Tannhäuser* and all about it and he said *Tannhäuser* had been his first opera, too, when he was just Graham's age, and they had a high time. So it was quite a day.

[A week or so later, the Baumgardts sent Graham a star map, which he used diligently in the wonderful sky-viewing opportunities of the farm. Professor Baumgardt died in the summer of 1963; Mrs. Fisher in 1958.]

June 16
There has been a frenzy of activity at the blockhouse the last couple of days. Yesterday, for a while, there were fifteen people working their simultaneously, counting us. Ann and I start moving in tonight. I've got a fellow coming with a truck and he and I will move all but a few pieces for which I shall have to get a mover in.

June 16 [from diary entry]
Beautiful day . . . In afternoon Mayville dropped in.

Went down to cove and discussed fencing and other plans.
Went to work at blockhouse getting ready for move. Water
working. Stove broken so will reject. Only two lights in
house. Fred Hutchins came with truck and I worked two and
a half hours with him moving. A shower blew up over mountains and lake and sprinkled us lightly. Then a magnificent
double rainbow, its entire arch visible, appeared in east and
remained for a half hour. A good omen and blessing on the
move. Finally quit at dark, very tired and came back up to
brick house for a snack.

July 9

. . . The other large operation was the putting up of my
electric fence, cutting the cattle out of our valuable wood lot.
It includes the main maple grove but also a lot of fine hem-
lock, pine, and oak. I still have more woods to fence off but
this was the most urgent job. I did it with Herbert, and
Frank, a Nyack boy who used to work for Mrs. Graham there
and is here for the summer. I've learned to use a post-hole
augur, which is a very gratifying instrument. The fence is
working first rate.

We've been having a spell of wonderful weather. Clear
days, hot in the sun, and downright cold at night. We've
been sleeping under two blankets. We've been swimming
and fishing and had a hot-dog roast on the beach while the
Michelmans were here. Fourth of July night the boys were
allowed to stay up to see fireworks visible across at Ticonderoga. We went to Burlington and bought a pasteurizer and
a churn. Ann now pasteurizes, after much policy discussion.
As soon as we are getting our full milk supply she will start
churning.

July 22

. . . I should have written sooner, and had the best of intentions, but of milking of cows there is no end and much pigs
are a weariness of the flesh . . .

August 3 [following an account of a jaunt to Ausable
        Chasm]

On the way back we came via Elizabethtown and recognized, from the pictures in our volume of the Hand letters,
Judge Augustus Hand's home in Elizabethtown. So we
stopped and trotted up to ask for the Judge, who it turned
out was just due to arrive later that afternoon from N. Y. on
his vacation. So we left our greeting and the suggestion that
he run over and see what has happened to the old home
place . . .

Oh, we have put forty pounds of beans in our freeze locker,
so far, and Ann and Virginia will begin canning tomatoes
soon. We are supplying all our own vegetables, now, in considerable variety and laying by a great deal by either canning
or freezing. All this is, of course, really vital to us if we expect
to eat next winter.

August 11 [includes an insight into the comings and goings
        of people]

Everything is terrifically active just now. Eighty-five acres
are being hayed, in fact are almost finished, and both our
barns are crammed with tons of baled hay. Next summer we
are going to take over some of that ourselves for it is a very
valuable crop and this way—the only way we can do this
summer, of course—we get a minimum return on it. Two
different farmers have it.

Also, Mrs. Graham has a really full house. The Diamonds, friends of our friends the Jacobses, are here for two weeks. Joe Reiner, one of the salesmen at Crown [the publisher I had been associated with], is here for two weeks with his wife and their daughter. John Scott and his wife and daughter were here overnight last night. Mary Abbot, my literary agent, and a friend of hers have just arrived for a week or so. Eleanor Deming, from New City, and a friend of hers were here overnight Monday. Another friend of Mary Abbot's is due for two weeks Friday, and Miss [Bert] Krantz is due for ten days Friday. All are very nice people. But you can imagine how things are humming and Virginia has her hands full.

Last Sunday night the Northern lights appeared brightly and were also visible Monday night. It is very impressive in this rather awesome setting and we are likely to see them frequently from now on through the fall and winter.

August 24

Yesterday was a notable day. Just after Ann's nap, as Ann and Bert and I were beginning to formulate a scheme, who should arrive, to our pleasure and astonishment, but Judge Augustus Hand and Mrs. Hand, returning our call from Elizabethtown. They were most gracious and delightful, the Judge of very impressive mien in the old tradition. He gets around slowly; he told me he is 79, but he is still as keen as ever on the bench. Mrs. Hand is a sprightly little old lady, of great charm. It was she who compiled and published the volume of the letters of the Hand family. They looked all over at everything we had done and were doing and expressed great approval and were very nice with the children.

Characteristic of her: I was standing, talking with the Judge, just before Ann came out, and Mrs. Hand had got

[41]

into a conversation with David. She pointed to her husband and said to David, "Just think of it, this old man's grandfather lived here." They stayed about an hour and a half and we had much interesting talk, touching on law and politics and many things other than the house. Then they departed with their chauffeur, inviting us to call at Elizabethtown. It was really a most happy experience and it meant a lot to us in our relation to the place.

The following spring Judge Hand wrote us a letter.

June 17, 1949

Dear Mr. Fuller:

It may interest you and your wife, as well as your mother-in-law, to see the following extract from a letter dated December 27, 1841, which was written by my great-grandfather Samuel Hand, who built the house at Shoreham you are living in, from which he moved to the brick house in 1841: "I have been much favored considering our great family and fatigue of body and mind, but we have been preserved thus far, and abandoned the old house last Thursday and have made a pretty good exchange for a cold day." From a calendar I find that December 27th in the year 1841 fell on Monday. Therefore it is evident that old Captain Hand moved out of the house you live in and into the brick house on Thursday, December 23, 1841.

With best wishes to all from my wife and myself, I am,

Sincerely yours,

(signed) Augustus N. Hand

A time was not long coming when Ann and I would heartily envy that "pretty good exchange for a cold day." As a point of interest on inflation, the Hand letters disclosed that the brick house and its outhouses were built for $1,200. We put upwards of $10,000 into improvements of it.

Such was the shape and tenor of a summer. Its greater, more unified dramas stand out alone.

I remarked earlier that Ann and I are peculiarly sensitive to aura—that subtle emanation that can be felt from places and objects heavily laden with significant associations. "George Washington slept here" became a stock phrase to the point of comedy in this country's quest for a sense of past. To tread where Christ had trod is the incentive of the pilgrim to the Holy Land. One walks with Cicero and Caesar in Rome.

As Vermont farms go, Hand's Cove had a remarkable aura. As farm buyers go, we were notably responsive to it. The place was rich in the sense of overlapping presences and large events. I was to look down often at the great lake, to swim in it, boat, fish, and skate on it, to fight its eroding force, and to wish I could tap its waters. During the seasons of open water it had a moderate traffic of barges and pleasure craft, but it had been the theatre of action for a long historical pageant involving great names in America's history.

The Indians had called it by a name which means "the gate of the country." The French explorer Samuel de Champlain had recognized that it was such a gate. In July of 1609 he sailed down it as far as Ticonderoga—and our farm—and supported his Algonquin friends in a skirmish with the Iroquois. That was about a month before Henry Hudson sailed up the river to the south that bears his name.

One of our earliest visitors, before we were fully unpacked, was my friend, the late Stewart Holbrook, sprightly historian and chronicler, a Vermonter turned Oregonian. He was astounded that we should have lit upon this spot. He prowled its shores with me. There, in the cove, Ethan Allen had rudely rejected the authority of Colonel Benedict Arnold, in the action against Ticonderoga, for although Vermont was fighting the British, she was also just about to declare herself a free and independent Republic.

"Colonel Allen, you curse most horrible," one of Ethan's foes once reproached him. It's quite likely that the cove resounded with those curses, some of them directed at Arnold. The Green Mountain Boys, known more vulgarly to the unadmiring as the Bennington Mob, were on the move.

Stewart and I talked of the Allen legend. He had studied it well in his biography, *Ethan Allen*. The schoolbook histories said that Ethan had called on the commander of Ti to surrender "in the name of the great Jehovah and the Continental Congress." Stewart contended that he had said, "Come out of there, you sons of British bitches." With Ethan's lifelong gift of natural rhetoric it is quite likely that he said both, for both are in his style.

It was an irony that just as we were settling *in*, Stewart was working on a piece of nineteenth-century social history, *The Yankee Exodus*, telling how a great migration of smart and energetic Vermonters had done just the opposite and got the hell *out*.

CHAPTER FIVE

Not So Deep As a Well

ALL OUR LIVES, water had been a commodity that came out of faucets, hot or cold.

When we bought the farm we were acutely, though naïvely, water-conscious, knowing enough to realize this was a major pitfall for the unwary. The owner, the neighboring farmers, and everyone else we consulted said there was a 250-foot artesian well. The owner had never put it to use because she had held the farm for such a brief tenure. Like the well on every farm that was ever put on the market it was called "never-failing."

Also, in our innocence, there was something reassuring about being right on the bank of Lake Champlain. It conveyed the notion that a 250-foot drilled well must tap the very sources of the lake itself.

Everyone did agree that the water would be hard. We had little practical experience of hard water and didn't think of it as a great problem. Much later, Dorothy Canfield Fisher told us the story of her great-grandmother Canfield coming into the valley at Arlington with her husband, looking for a place to settle. She carried a linen handkerchief and a piece of homemade soap. Whenever she came to a stream or pond she hopped out of the wagon and tried the water. When she found a fine stream at Arlington with water that lathered abundantly enough to pass her test, the Canfield farm was settled in that lovely, historic valley.

Our brick house was about six hundred feet, the block-house eight hundred, distant from the well. The idea was that a pump installed at the wellhead would serve both houses and the barns to boot. As I've noted, each house had a rain-water cistern with a hand pump in the kitchen and we planned to make do with these until the large project could be completed.

Getting bids and the advice that went with them was a tricky business which we approached with trepidation. Here, too, we could go wrong in big and costly ways. We had been warned against shrewd Yankee traders who might sell us sky funnels to catch hurricanes. Moreover, there was current in the town, probably inevitably, the notion that the new people from New York who had bought the Hand farm—the man a writing feller—were rolling in money. It was held to be demonstrably true. Were we not putting in water and electricity and heat? The narrow margin on which these staggering but necessary operations were calculated, and the gamble they represented to a man who had thrown up a good position and sunk everything he had in something he knew virtually nothing about, was something they could not imagine. But we slept with this awareness. And we eyed all counselors and bidders warily.

Mr. Gregoire, a plumbing contractor in the village, had been recommended. I liked him on sight and felt inclined to trust him. Though his name testified to French-Canadian origins, by adaptation he was a walking map of Vermont: white-haired, weathered, direct, and possessed of a dry wit. Not until I got the first bill did I discover how his name was spelled, for it was universally pronounced Gregwire. The children called him Mr. McGregor for a while, insisting that he looked like the pictures of that dangerous gardener in Beatrix Potter's *Tale of Peter Rabbit.*

Gregoire knew the property and thought he knew the well. There would be plenty of water, he was sure, but it would be hard. Before I had concluded anything with him on the big job, we needed new leathers for the kitchen pump. These are gaskets of a sort that hold the vacuum in a pipe in which a long column of water is being lifted. If they are dried and cracked, as ours were, the pump won't work. Like parts to Model-T Fords, such things were becoming hard to get. In search of these, at a neighbor's suggestion, I sought out Mr. Sims, another plumber in the village. I found him in a large messy workshop behind his house. He was startled by my abrupt entrance—by anybody's entrance, I gather—and I think he stashed away a bottle hastily. He shuffled forward with a furtive air and scrutinized me coldly.

I introduced myself. He eyed me for a while and finally admitted that he knew of the farm that I claimed to have bought.

Would he come down and put leathers in the pump for me?

"I guess so," he said after another wait. "People around here, when they've got a ten-cent job they give it to me. When they've got a big job they give it to somebody else."

I smelled the reason on his breath. I did not warm to Mr. Sims, but I reminded myself that a comparative bid would be helpful.

"I'm planning to put in a water system," I said. "Do you want to bid on it?"

"I'll bid on it," he said in his surly way.

"Now I figured," I went on, "that the two-hundred-and-fifty-foot artesian well would be able to take care of both houses."

He gave me a quick sharp glance. "Who told you it was two hundred and fifty feet?"

"Well," I said, disconcerted, "that was what I understood when I bought the place. Everybody around seems to agree that that's how deep it is—everybody who knows the place."

"It's not more'n a hundred and fifty feet," he asserted flatly.

"Are you sure?"

"I ought to know," he said. "I had the pipe out of it a couple of years ago. It's a hundred and fifty feet."

"Well, does that matter?" I asked uncertainly. "Do you think it'll be enough water?"

"Don't know," he said. "Have to test the rate of flow."

I left, perturbed in spirit. It was agreed that Mr. Sims would study the problem and make a bid. I never saw him again, ever, drunk or sober. He never came to me and I never went back to him. The leathers were put in the pump by Mr. Gregoire, with whom I now took up the depth question. "What about this? Sims says it's a hundred and fifty feet."

"Well, now, I don't know," Mr. Gregoire admitted. "I always thought it was around two hundred and fifty. Anyway, they always had plenty of water. They used to have a gravity line running down to a tub in the barnyard. Of course we'll haul it up and see."

I went down to the low pump house. The hand pump that now capped the well was powerful and shot a strong jet through a short length of hose attached to it. I filled a pail to see if the cloudiness I had noted in the water previously had settled. It had not. This troubled me. But the men who were working around it drank it, and everyone said the water had always been good, so the cloudiness was attributed to long disuse of the pump and the well. "It will pump out," everyone agreed. "There's nothing the matter with that water except it's hard."

On a Sunday afternoon a car drove in and a stranger got out. He introduced himself as Ralph Bunyan, from one of the larger towns north of us. He didn't seem particularly happy in his identity. There was a discouraged and lugubrious air about him.

"I hear you're putting in a water system," he said.

"That's right."

"I'd like to bid on it."

"I'll be glad to have you estimate it," I said. "Several others are doing so, and I'll say frankly that I've almost concluded to give it to Gregoire, but I'll wait for your bid."

Bunyan launched into a bitter denunciation of Gregoire and every other plumber in western Vermont, with case histories and lavish details. When he had finished he looked down toward the well and shook his head gloomily.

"Oh," he said, "this water here! I know all about it."

"What do you mean?" I asked fearfully.

"It's so hard I don't guess there's much can be done with it. It fills pipe up solid. Why, that line they had running down to the barn—they had to put that in new every three years. I know because I sold 'em the pipe for it."

"I didn't think it was as hard as that," I muttered.

Bunyan moaned slightly and wagged his head. "This water

by the lake! Why, right down here about two miles south there was a fellow sent a sample from his well to a softener company for analysis. They sent it back and said there wasn't any such water. He finally had to send it all the way to Texas for analysis, and you know what that water was? Pure Epsom salts!"

I stood speechless.

"It was just right down here a ways," he added. "Of course you'll have to use all copper pipe . . . if you can get it. Have you had it analyzed yet for pollution?"

"No," I said. "Do you want to take a sample?"

"No," he said sorrowfully. "You'll have to have an official jug."

He departed, agreeing to come within the next few days to test the rate of flow. Five minutes later he drove in again. "Guess I will take a sample," he said. He offered no further explanation and I was too depressed to ask for one.

We went down and filled a quart jar with its cloudy best. He departed. I never saw him again, either. I often wondered if he had drunk the sample and died of it.

The next morning I mentioned him to Gregoire, who simply said, "God help you!" and made no further comment. But Gregoire was beginning to worry about the water. He opened up the top of the well and pulled up the pipe and also dug up some of the old line to the barn. He called me down to see it.

"It's worse than I thought," he admitted.

I saw a two-inch pipe, filled up with an ugly, heavy mineral deposit so that scarcely a pencil-breadth of opening remained. My heart quailed.

"What about copper pipe?"

"Nope. I still say, if we could use this water at all that inch-

and-a-quarter iron pipe would be as good as smaller copper. But I'm afraid of this with anything. I didn't realize it was this bad. I'm losing sleep thinking about what it will do to interior plumbing. And as for a hot water system . . . !"

I gazed at him mutely.

"Another thing," he went on while I was absorbing the matter of the pipe, "this well isn't any two hundred and fifty feet or hundred and fifty feet, either. It's forty feet, and the first fourteen of it is a dug well."

"But Sims said he put in a hundred and fifty feet of pipe."

"Not unless he squeezed it down to forty feet, he didn't."

Clinging tenaciously to this wretched hole in the ground I asked, "Will it be enough?"

"Well, nobody around here seems to have heard about it ever going dry. There's a steady overflow here. But with a power pump on it and a long dry spell, I wouldn't know."

We agreed that an analysis was necessary anyway. An official jug was obtained from the Department of Health in Burlington and sent in with a request for a complete analysis of mineral content. The report was received in a week with no analysis for mineral content but with the terse comment: "Contains stomach bacteria. Unfit for human consumption."

That was the end of the well.

It was appalling. We were right where we thought it was impossible to be—high and dry beside a vast body of water.

I had had time to learn some things and to reach some conclusions. We knew, by now, that water was notoriously a problem all along the lake. Nobody had ever told us, and like the man who unwittingly married the snake charmer, we had never asked.

If I'd read all of the Hand letters by then, I'd have found we were far from the first to have such troubles, on the testimony of the two gallant maiden ladies who managed the farm during much of the late nineteenth century. Susan Hand wrote on September 12, 1874: ". . . we . . . must shingle leaking roofs, find water for choking cattle . . . these are wants and evils of long standing and must be attended to or there will be much waste and suffering."

Another thing I realized was that there had been no bad faith, no deliberate misrepresentation. In all likelihood there seldom is. The owner told us what she thought. She did not really know, had never put it to the test, but thought that other people knew. So did everyone we asked. They had heard, or "known," or always understood that it was thus and so.

We wanted the farm, still wanted it, would have bought it anyway, no doubt—but what the devil we were going to do about water was another question. The idea of a central system was abandoned. Each house was on its own.

Virginia's needs at the brick house were more urgent, for reasons of summer business, than ours in the frame house. By now we had been there several weeks. Spring was well advanced. Being a purposeful and ingenious woman, Virginia thought of a solution that might take care of her needs. She had a large cistern to collect the rain water from the house. The big old sheep barn, a few hundred feet away, had an enormous cistern, long in disuse. Susan and Eliza Hand had written on November 19, 1875: "We have been building a cement cistern in a sheep shed and have encountered manifold difficulties in getting workmen and materials . . ."

By cleaning out this, equipping the barn with eave spouts, and running a pipe line to the house, both cisterns were made available and the combined water-collecting capacity was considerable. Except in case of phenomenal drought, this seemed adequate, even for bathroom plumbing, and accordingly we carried out the scheme. The conception was much admired by Mr. Gregoire.

Ann and I, destined to live in the blockhouse, were still left with an unsolved problem. It had to be solved, somehow, sometime, so to avoid later delay we went ahead quixotically and had a bathroom and a kitchen sink put in, and ran everything for the time being on our rain-water cistern, which had a peak capacity of fifteen hundred gallons and a small roof area from which to collect water.

Then we began to learn some of the arithmetic of water, unknown to those living in citified luxury. Naturally, a cistern is not maintained at full capacity. Now we learned that each time a toilet is flushed it uses from six to eight gallons of water. A family of five, with city habits, would flush a toilet at a minimum of fifteen times daily. Without accounting for any other use of water, that is a matter of a hundred gallons or so. Kitchen and washing use must be reckoned, and drinking—but that hundred gallons for the toilet alone could finish us because the rains, on which we depended for replenishment, were never of the intensity to fill the cistern completely in one storm.

One of our neighbors, a re-educated city person, said, "Good heavens! Do you flush the toilet every time it's used? You'll find you can't do that." So we set about the task of breaking down toilet disciplines that had been instilled carefully into our children in our city days, and we began brushing our teeth out of tumblers.

But our water system at the blockhouse would also have to supply the cattle barn. This could accommodate twenty-six head of milking cattle, plus young stock. We were already arranging to board quite a few heifers the following winter, plus a cow of our own. What were they to drink? A cow, we learned, will drink about six gallons of water daily.

Now, every few days, councils of war were held. There was the question of sinking a new well, beside the house. This was put aside on the probability of spending a great deal of money and having nothing to show for it but rock dust or Epsom salts. Gregoire, inspired by the solution at the brick house, spoke wistfully of a big cistern to gather from the immense watershed of the cow barn. But he recalled, and a later pipe-laying operation confirmed, that the barn sat upon a slate ledge. Moreover, even a very big cistern would not solve the future cattle problem, and a farm that could not water cattle would be no farm. Was it worth while using the old well solely for the barn, as had been done in times past?

Meanwhile, in spite of cautious husbandry, the level in the blockhouse cistern fell, and the sun shone in cloudless skies, as in *The Ancient Mariner*. I removed the lid of the cistern and lowered a line, one morning, to discover that only a foot of water was left. A man in the village, named Jimmy Fuller —no kin—operated a shiny milk-tank truck. I phoned him and threw myself at his mercy. "As one Fuller to another, can you bring me a load of water?"

"Well, maybe I can tonight, around ten o'clock, when I get back from my run. But it'll be awful hard water, from the milk plant."

"Never mind," I said. "Any water that's clean."

Our visitors at the time, among the earliest of Virginia's customers, were my friend Herbert Michelman, from my former office, and his wife. They were appalled and fascinated by the situation. We were all together that evening when the silvery bulk of the tank truck came rumbling down. Jimmy Fuller backed up close to the cistern top and dropped in a nozzle. Water began flowing with an ominous booming, re-verberating splash into the black, seemingly fathomless depths. We brought flashlights and watched the gradual filling, the thick jet of water was silvery in the light beams. But as I leaned over the cistern, the huge bulk of the truck looming over me, a fearsome odor smote my nostrils.

I look up in alarm. This was supposed to be a milk tank that had been washed out with steam.

"It smells like fuel oil," I said.

Jimmy Fuller laughed raucously. "Brother, that's hard water! You think it *smells* like fuel oil! It's all right if its cold, but don't ever taste it when it's warm."

Thus hard water came to us without benefit of well. We were glad enough to have it, but it was weeks before it was gradually purged out of the cistern by cumulative rainfall. It had to be paid for, of course, though I forget how much, as my unconscious was determined to bury the whole business.

Our water operations were followed intently by the town. What the odds were for or against us I can't say, but curiosity and speculation ran high. One townsman—fat and gossipy—came down with a truckload of lumber and insulation, for in that simultaneity of which I spoke, the water job was not the only one under way. Ann came downstairs to speak with him. As she went through the dining room she glanced out the window and caught the townsman surreptitiously lifting up the cistern lid and peering in, looking for news to report. She let the back door slam as she came out, and when she appeared around the corner he was leaning casually against the cistern top, studying the flight of a bird.

Meanwhile Lake Champlain's beautiful waters rippled placidly as we deliberated. Gregoire and I were now thinking of it as a source. It was possible to pump water from the lake;

some places did it; but we were a good twelve hundred feet from the nearest water's edge and there were other complications. Lake Champlain erodes its shoreline murderously wherever it is anything other than rocks and woods. Our great promontory of pasture land extending out into the lake was eroded spectacularly on the north side. Allen Mayville, head of the U.S. Soil Conservation District, was helping us make long-range plans to check this condition, along with other projects for the farm. One time we touched on the subject of water, and he said, "Why don't you build a pond?"

I scouted the idea irritably. "I am certainly not going to sit on the banks of the lake and build a pond."

When I told him of the collapse of the well hopes, he broached the matter of a pond again. The scheme had no appeal to me whatever. "I just don't like the idea," I protested. "It seems downright foolish to build a pond beside a lake."

But the lake was next eliminated as a source. It would be an extensive trenching and pipe-laying operation to reach it. Walt Bryant, who owned the trench digger, looked over the lay of the land and frowned upon the prospects. The bank, at all the nearest points to the house, rose some twenty feet or more over the water and was subject to constant crumbling and shifting. He would not guarantee any pipe line from being carried away in the spring breakup.

"You'd be better off building a pond," he counseled.

Gregoire, who had shared my reluctance, finally concurred. I surrendered my opposition and the project was launched. By this time we were desperate for water, anywhere and anyhow. The homely joy of the running tap was now appreciated by us in all its wonder.

The pond was a triple play. Allen Mayville's federal conservation office provided the meticulous engineering free of charge: a service the value of which became ever more and more impressed upon us. Walt Bryant would build it. Gregoire would pipe it to the house.

Once we were committed to the operation, it began to take on an intense excitement for Ann and me. The pond was to fit into a natural hollow of the land not more than a hundred feet behind the house. A sharp slope drained about ten acres of pasture into this. The natural hill would provide two sides of a long, roughly rectangular pond; and a dam would provide the other two sides. The whole thing would be fashioned from the basic Vergennes clay, heavy and nonporous, which was the major component of the soil of our region. It is rich and good, of its kind, excellent for apple orchards and grass alike, but hard to work; and when wet, it is impassable, immovable, and impossible.

There was a phase of surveying and plan drawing. Finally the approved plans came down from Montpelier, where they had been sent to pass a state inspection required for any pond formed by impounding rather than by digging.

Just as darkness was falling one evening a heavy trailer came rolling in, bearing the ponderous, thirteen-ton bulldozer. The next morning it coughed and roared its way into life and began what had by now come to seem to us the mightiest work of man since the Panama Canal.

The master of this machine was a short, heavy man of abundant geniality and good nature, called Stubby. For several days it seemed as though he did nothing but push earth around from one place to another. He was, in fact, scraping off and shoving back the porous topsoil against the time it would be returned as top dressing for the finished dam.

When it set at the main task of hollowing out the bed of

the pond and forming the massive dam, the bulldozer really displayed its powers. We watched in fascination as it repeatedly raised its blade, slammed it down to take a bite from the dense clay mass and with a stupendous, bellowing VRRRRR-OOOOOOOOOOOMMMMM! lumbered forward with it against all probability. It would climb the ever-rising bank, shoving the accumulating load, hover at the stall point, then teeter over the crest, backing and filling, up, down, and across the slope in apparent imminent danger of capsizing.

Stubby was almost a part of the machine, centaur-like. His short, chunky body sat unmoving and erect on the large padded seat, never affected in its equilibrium by shock or careen, impervious to the demoniacal roar. His manipulation of the complex controls was calm and assured, and he seemed possessed by a stolid exultation. About two thirds of a cigar, generally unlit, projected straight from the center of his mouth and created a bizarre parody of the famous painting of Brahms at the piano. Stubby, too, was a virtuoso.

Walt Bryant himself, even though he was the owner of the machine, was not immune to its spell. On his trips down to inspect the progress, he would stand and watch it for a long time, motionless, his face fearsomely screwed up in an unconscious ecstasy of concentration.

Shortly before this die was cast, Ann had discovered in the works of Louis Bromfield, the laureate of agriculture, a fascinating discourse on the life cycle of a farm pond. This opened our eyes to the varying forms of excitement the project would hold for us long after its construction was finished, and quite apart from the utilitarian concern that had launched it.

Under the influence of these widening perspectives, I had stood enthralled during the last part of the planning stage when all of us, unspokenly, were permitting the enterprise to grow to a scale far bigger than that first contemplated—and far more expensive. We had become obsessed with water to such a degree that I could have agreed to the construction of a second Lake Champlain. I wanted lots of water—inexhaustible water. And I wanted a pond that would lead a life of its own and not be a mere storage hole in the ground.

As for the conservation people and Walt, they became filled with the zeal of constructing what was by far the largest and most elaborate pond ever created in the district. By dint of having a surface area of three tenths of an acre, it became eligible for government fish stocking with a balanced population of largemouth black bass and bluegill sunfish. This whetted my appetite, in spite of all the fish in Lake Champlain, and I began reading Department of Agriculture publications on fish as a crop, otherwise known as pisciculture. The climax of this phase was reached when a visiting higher-up of the conservation service said to me, "What we worry about, Mr. Fuller, with conservation-minded people, is that you won't fish it hard enough."

I received from my mother, at about this time, a clipping with pictures of a Maryland farm being rebuilt from the ground up, houses and all, a pond constructed, and so forth, all free, as a government demonstration. In her letter she said, "I wish the government would do this for you. If they do it in Maryland, why wouldn't they do it in Vermont?" This vexed me out of all rational proportion and I replied irritably that the government was already doing a great deal for me.

The work was finished under the tension of threatening weather. Being desperate for water, we prayed for rain lest we be forced to buy another truckload of aromatic spirits of fuel oil, but if it came in abundance a day or so too soon, it would ruin the conclusion of the work. It sprinkled, tentatively, but held off. Stubby pushed the flanking mounds of topsoil up on top of the finished dam, and with the infinite delicacy of a mother stroking her baby's brow, spread it thinly and evenly over the top and sides. From the appalling mess of the first few days had emerged an impressive structure of the utmost neatness and precision.

The next day it began raining in earnest. Noah himself had not made his deadline more opportunely. Walt and Allen came down and stood with me on top of the dam, watching the caterpillar tracks on the clay bottom disappearing under the widening brown pool. Walt said, "I'll be surprised if you ever see the bottom of that again."

It rained pretty steadily for three days and nights. I was astonished at the volume of the flow into the pond from the high ground of the upper pasture. It entered the pond with considerable roar and rush. Ann and I could not keep our minds from it. We were constantly peering out the windows or journeying over to observe its progress. At night, after the last of the chores were finished, we went in our raincoats and boots through the pouring rain and gummy mud to watch, with flashlights, the furious flow and to note the steadily rising level.

When the rains stopped, the water had already come within three or four inches of the top of the trickle pipe, designed to maintain a maximum level under normal conditions. This meant that there was eight feet of water throughout the greater part of the pond. The estimated volume was approximately six hundred thousand gallons.

For a few days the water was a muddy brown, but then it rapidly settled and cleared. The jet pump was suspended from a pole below the freeze depth near the center—one of

Gregoire's men swimming out with it—and our do-it-yourself, never-failing water supply went into use. We did not drink it, nor use it in the hot-water system. For these purposes the cistern was adequate. But in an intricate linkage the pond maintained our toilet on city standards, provided the cold water for the bathtub, and was run over to the barn-yard, where it supplied a large drinking tub for cattle. Yet for all its abundance, it picked up alkalis from the soil and was hard. From alkalis and pond algae it smelled high as it ran from the taps. In the bathtub it was the brownish color of the peaty streams of the Scottish highlands, and the addition of hot water brought out its rich effluvia.

Now it was already autumn, but despite the lateness of the season we seeded down at least a portion of the dam, for though neat, it had a naked look. The program was elaborate: continued planting until a good grassy bank was established, especially a firm sod at the low dip designed as a spillway if the trickle pipe were overtaxed. Shrubs and a few trees were to follow. Not only the bank but even the water were to be fertilized to promote the growth of vegetation necessary for the fish with which the pond was to be stocked.

We did not have to wait long for the appearance of life forms. A few small black water bugs appeared, and then came the frog invasion. The surrounding meadows harbored many bright-green frogs. Hundreds of these now congregated at the pond and formed a ring around its edge, partly in and partly out of the water. The boys, accompanied by a young police dog we had acquired during the summer, loved to dash madly around the edge, starting this frog populace on a furious splashing and diving for safety. The place was theirs until predatory birds and the coming fish would establish a balance.

I caught a wood turtle and introduced it into the pond; it

would not remain, however, since the wood turtle is primarily a landlubber. But the common eastern painteds were sure to settle. We were warned to be on guard against muskrats venturing up from the cove, for they would be harmful to the dam.

One day the children set up a holler. We rushed out. Along the edge of the alfalfa meadow, headed for the dam, a monstrous snapping turtle stalked, holding himself high, his shell more than a foot long. It was the largest we had ever seen, though by no means a true giant of its baleful kind. It plodded with the imperturbable determination of all turtles, clearly seeming to sense the new pond in some mysterious way.

This was a tenant we did not want, though how long we could hope to exclude the species was a question. They prey on ducks, among other things, seizing the innocent swimmers by the foot and dragging them down to doom.

The turtle would not stop. If one stood in front of it, it kept coming, the massive head with its razor beak jutting fiercely from the thick leathery neck. It was discretion to step aside.

Our friend Harley Cook, an aging, archetypal Vermonter, was doing some carpentry for us. He came to see the fuss and laid claim to the creature, as we had no culinary plans for it, due to inexperience and timidity. We were awed when Harley stooped swiftly and snatched up the heavy, ugly monster by the thick tail. A snapper's jaws can reach anything anywhere on its shell. It cannot reach its tail—barely. The great head, hissing and snapping fearsomely, lashed about as Harley held the turtle at arm's length so it could not bite his legs. Destined for the soup kettle, it was dumped in the trunk of Harley's car. Unlovable though it was, Meredith shed a few tears for it. Esmé Cook sent down a jar of the soup a day later, and those who tasted it found it delicious.

On a clear afternoon Ann and I sat down briefly on the bank. It was our good luck that a large kingfisher swooped over repeatedly, and one of the several white egrets that summered on the lakeshore made low runs over the surface, on reconnaissance missions. They were a bit premature—no pickings, except for small frogs. Next year, perhaps.

Water could never be the same to us—never casual again. We had become acutely conscious of its waste, of the harmfulness of letting it get out of hand, of how it will vanish when squandered, of how it will depart when the woods have gone, and come back when they return.

We read an item in the paper about the lowered water table on some part of the West Coast leading to the invasion of wells and springs by salt water, and we said, like the scriptural horses, "Ha! Ha!"

A long drought in late autumn reduced the pond's level not more than four inches, in spite of continuous use. The heavy rains of the early winter caused it to pour through the trickle pipe with the sound of a Titan sucking his teeth. It froze at capacity, heavily, and at Christmastime we were all skating on it. It was a superb rink, smooth as glass, easily cleared of light snow, handy to the house when the cold winds were roaring, and flanked by woods and meadows, lake and mountains.

It was not even so deep as the abandoned well, but it served. And who ever heard of fishing and skating in a well?

CHAPTER SIX

The Backsliding Heifer

ALTHOUGH I AM NOT without courage in some matters, much of my life I have been timid about big animals, largely through lack of experience with them. When we decided to move to the farm we had planned from the first to have a cow sooner or later, though we hadn't projected much beyond that point. Clearly it was necessary to know how to milk before getting a cow. Learning to milk was the supreme symbol of the New Way of Life. It had ritual value and he who milked would be high priest of our farm. In all my life I had never touched a cow or seen one closer than over a pasture fence.

When we were settled in, I said to my young neighbor Paul, who had taken over his father's farm, "Look, frankly I am afraid of cows—in the sense that I don't know anything about them and have never been near them. But I want to learn to handle them and how to milk. Please teach me."

Paul said, "Okay. Come around at milking time."

A few days elapsed before honor pricked me on and I turned up at Paul's barn for the afternoon milking. The idea was that I should just hang around, observe operations, get used to the cows, and let them get used to me. Also there was the matter of getting used to the wholesome, robust, but initially overwhelming fragrances of the barn.

Paul's herd was Holstein, like most of those in our section of Vermont. One of these is a lot of animal. Cows are keenly aware of strangers. I walked up and down the aisles gingerly, keeping my distance from the shifting hind feet, while Paul explained helpfully, in response to my question, that yes, all farmers got kicked from time to time, especially in the winter when the cows were restless. I was glad it was summer. His father, Paul went on, had twice had his leg broken by kicks— it's possible, but I suspect he was laying it on for my benefit.

For several days I observed, doing minor chores for which I was not needed, such as emptying milk pails through the strainer into the cans. Then, without warning, as I stood idly by, Paul removed the milking machines from one of the cows and said, "Ed, do you want to strip this cow?"

"Uh . . . why, yes," I said.

Determined but alarmed, I sat down on the three-legged stool beside the cow, which loomed immense over me.

"Closer," Paul said, giving me a helpful shove. I felt surrounded, looking up at a vast ceiling of cow belly, at the same time nervously conscious of another shuffling beast directly behind me.

I grasped the front teats, momentarily squeamish at the warmth and leathery toughness of them. Gingerly I gave a squeeze and was rewarded immediately by feeling the distinct flow of the milk—but *upward*.

"It's going back into the bag," Paul said. "You've got to choke it off at the top. And don't wrap your fingers all the way around, cramp them halfway."

I experimented, and extracted one or two vigorous squirts, the cow meanwhile leaning ponderously against me as if suddenly discovering a way to take the load off her feet. On one of my best tries I allowed the teat to bend in my hand and a warm, fragrant jet shot squarely up the inside of my sleeve, wetting me to the elbow. At last I gave up, and Paul stripped the cow with a few forceful pulls.

"I'm afraid to squeeze too hard," I said. "I'm afraid I'll hurt her."

"Don't worry," Paul said. "You can't."

The next day, in the miraculous transformation that marks the acquiring of all special knacks, I mastered the grip. It appeared to be second nature from then on—I could scarcely repeat the incorrect holds of before. But still I had not acquired the strength and vigor to complete the stripping.

Within a few days Paul transferred me to the complete operation of hand milking a Guernsey, kept to bring up the butterfat average of the herd. Proudly I succeeded in milking her bone-dry—but not without a new development. Halfway through the task, the weight of the big stainless-steel milk pail gripped between my knees became insupportable. My weary legs began to tremble so violently that the milk sloshed over and I was reduced to the bad practice of resting the pail on the floor. This also passed off in a day or so. The stiff hands and wrists I had been told to expect from milking never developed, probably because one who has pounded millions of words out of a typewriter by the touch system develops finger and wrist muscles. I'm sure a good pianist could milk, too.

It became a regular routine for me to milk the Guernsey.

As the elementary grips and techniques were mastered I had to face the secondary problems. The second time that my legs failed and I set the milk pail on the floor, the cow promptly put her foot in it, splashing me all over with milk and kicking the bucket all the way backward across the aisle where it agitated the Holsteins who clattered it about until Paul charged in and retrieved it.

Mopped off but smelling like a nursing mother, I sat down with a clean pail to try again, having lost roughly half the evening's output. The cow, edified and entertained by her success, was trying for two in a row. The moment I touched her teats the big leg came up, probing forward and knocking me backward on the stool.

"You've gotta lean into her and block that kick," Paul said, and as before, he shoved me into position unceremoniously.

This was more of a bodily-contact sport than I reckoned. I had to brace my left shoulder hard against the haunch, like a schoolboy football player bucking the practice blocking sled. The idea was to prevent a kick from starting. Instead of reaching straight under for the udder, I had to huddle into that haunch, my left arm curved awkwardly and wearyingly so that I could reach the teat but could also brace the arm against an attempted kick. To do this at all took practice; to do it without letting go, still more. I mastered it sufficiently so that the Guernsey figured the percentages were against her and stopped trying.

I simply had not the weight or muscle, or above all the know-how, to work this maneuver against a determined Holstein, as I discovered when Paul set me to further stripping. The smaller Jerseys are easier to handle—a fact which influenced our own acquisitions as much as the higher butterfat count.

· · ·

We had been advised to buy a first-calf heifer: that is, a heifer about to freshen for the first time. A heifer graduates to cow status upon the birth of her third calf. Not being so brash as to shop unaided, I persuaded Paul to accompany me on the search for a suitable Jersey first-calf heifer. Late in June, on a rainy morning when the haying was at a standstill, I set forth with Paul, Graham, and David.

"I know I can't hold you responsible," I said to Paul, "but the one thing I ask is, don't let me buy anything that you wouldn't buy for your own herd."

So began a round of auction barns and dealers while Paul held forth instructively, under my barrage of questions, about the old-time let-the-buyer-beware traditions of the cattle market. It still stands as the rule of the trade that anything the dealer can pass off on you, living or dead, is fair game. If the cow has mastitis—a disease of the udder—the dealer will say she hasn't, and if you cannot discern it you have no comeback. Fear of mastitis had become obsessive with me as the result of reading a wealth of instructive and terrifying government literature.

We were not looking for pedigreed stock but for an acceptable "grade," as unregistered cattle are called. The one heifer we found that looked good to me Paul dismissed: "Too beefy." At last we tried the farm of a dealer named Rob Allen, near Vergennes. He was a bluff, hearty soul, red-faced, large-framed, and loud-voiced. Upon hearing our story he said, "Oh, I've got a nice little heifer out here—just what you're looking for."

We trooped out to the pasture. Rummaging among the variegated herd, he pointed out an unprepossessing, dun-colored little creature with a pair of sharp horns.

"Oh," I said in dismay, "I don't think I ought to get one with horns. The children, you know."

Everyone agreed that this was nothing. They could be cut off in the autumn after the flies were gone. "We'll take her into the barn," Allen said heartily, "and you can look her over better. She'll make you a nice little family cow. I'd buy her myself if I was looking for one."

"She's pretty runty," Paul observed on the way to the barn. My discouragement deepened.

In the barn she was too small to be held by the stanchions built for mature Holsteins, and wandered from one to another. Yet, somehow, a mysterious change that I cannot account for came over the psychological climate. Inexplicably I felt that I was fated to have this heifer and none other. We cornered her and Paul began a mysterious investigation, "punching the calf," poking at curious holes and joints, rubbing and feeling her all over.

"These here little cows," Rob Allen was saying, "can give an awful lot of milk. More'n the big ones sometimes. And of course—she was bred at eighteen months, which was a little too soon, 'cause she's undersized anyway, but I think she'll make a nice gentle little family cow."

"She's got a good milk well," Paul said.

"When will she have her calf?"

"Oh, she'll freshen in about a week or ten days."

"She's Jersey, isn't she?"

"Mostly, mostly," Allen said. "Oh, I think she's got a little Guernsey in her, but it's a good combination."

"Was she bred to a Jersey bull?"

"I think so," he said. "I'm not sure. I bought her from a feller in Connecticut that has Jerseys. I think she was bred to a Jersey bull. Of course, I've only had her about ten days."

We closed the deal for a hundred and twenty-five dollars. I felt sure that Paul wouldn't have taken her for his own herd as a gift.

Allen delivered Susan—a name we had selected in advance —a few days later, leaving her at Paul's barn, for she was to stay with his herd until she had her calf. Then the dealer came on down to pick up his check.

"You think she's going to be a good cow?" Ann asked.

"Oh yes, oh yes!" he cried cheerily. "She's little, but she's milky."

On the Fourth of July my friend Ira Payne, a fine printer I had known in my publishing days, came to see our farm. He was one of the leading breeders of Jerseys in America and the owner of Borden's "Elsie." I led him out to the pasture to see Susan.

"Well," he said in a kindly way, "she hasn't got much Jersey in her."

"What is she?" I asked.

"Mostly Guernsey," he said, but being a man of great consideration, then proceeded to gentle me up with encouraging words, looking toward the best.

On our way back, we met Paul and Graham. I introduced Payne and said, "He thinks she's mostly Guernsey."

Paul made a noncommittal sound.

"I think she's going to have that calf before morning," Mr. Payne said, citing anatomical pieces of evidence that were beyond me.

Paul listened but was evidently nettled by the prognostications of what he took to be a city man. He remarked aside to Graham as we departed, "That man don't know anything about cows. She won't have that calf for a week," a verdict on which Graham decided to rest his faith.

Susan had the calf before morning. When Paul sent down word I crowed over Graham but instructed him not to crow over Paul. Our entire family made a pilgrimage to the far pasture. It was a wet, overcast day, and we were variously attired and booted and filled with elation. When we reached the fence corner to which she had withdrawn, Susan was lying down, the calf curled up beside her, no bigger than a half-grown setter. To everyone's astonishment it looked to be pure Ayrshire, white and brown.

Susan scrambled up warily as we approached. The calf tottered to its feet. Susan nuzzled and licked it caressingly, uttering gentle lowing sounds. Our hearts melted.

"It's a heifer calf," Paul said.

We rejoiced. It had been predetermined that in this event she should be called Daisy and be raised as a second milch cow—an ominously overenthusiastic departure from the original plan to keep one family cow for our own milk supply.

The journey back to the barn was long. Part of the way Daisy wobbled along under her own steam, looking like a fugitive from the Disney studios. Susan followed, lowing comments of concern and disapproval. At times I carried Daisy around my neck like a fur piece, biblical-shepherd style, and felt like a walking illustration from a Sunday School paper. Susan, at these intervals, would become confused and bolt off rearward under the impression that her baby had been left behind. We had to round her up and let her sniff the calf to reorient her.

Then mother and child were transferred from Paul's to rattle around in our own big barn under our own care. This filled us with a portentous sense of challenge and responsibility only one remove from bringing a first baby home from hospital. I fixed up a special stanchion, narrowed with a board, to fit Susan, the original having been tailored to full-scale Holstein size. Ann took over Daisy. I took over Susan. The critters were definitely a part of the family.

We separated the calf from Susan on the third day and were upset by the cries and laments of both. I built a small pen near Susan's stanchion and she was occasionally indulged by a chance to lick Daisy with her great curling tongue, and murmur to her.

Susan milked easily and was docile. Her production began at seven or eight quarts a day, which was mighty small but was supposed to build up. To my alarm it went down, sharply. From day to day it diminished toward the trickle point. At the same time she began to cough—a fine, racking cough.

I looked dubiously at the Vermont tuberculin-test tag on her ear, fearing she should more appropriately have been named Camille, and called the vet. Dr. Miller came and diagnosed shipping fever, a bovine equivalent of distemper usually picked up in the careless shuttling of dealer-traded stock. Before our heartsick gaze he slipped an ice-tong-like contraption into her nostrils, tied her head up high at the stanchion, and set to work. He pumped a quart of something into her intravenously; rammed several golf-ball-sized sulfa pills down her throat at one time with a gadget that looked like a mixture of blowgun, slide trombone, and pinball shooter; and finished by injecting penicillin into her shoulder. He departed, guaranteeing nothing.

I nursed Susan like my own flesh and blood; coddled her, grained her, medicated her, and hoped for the best. She pulled through, and under heavy feeding the milk production gradually returned and went up to eight quarts, where it remained. Under the new circumstances, what had seemed like little now seemed like a lot.

Ann had the large task of weaning Daisy—converting her from liquid to solid propellant. Before that, she coped with teaching her to drink milk from a pail as soon as she was removed from Susan.

Ann began with a special nursing pail we had seen in the stores but her experience supported the farmers' disdain for it. From the base of an ordinary bucket a fat rubber teat projected ludicrously. Ann put fresh warm milk in the pail and tried to induce Daisy to suck. No dice. She wanted to nuzzle under the mother and butt the bag—an astonishing performance that appalled us when we first saw it and illuminated my silly fear of hurting the cow when milking. Possibly Daisy didn't care for the taste or texture of the rubber either.

From necessity Ann fell back upon the farmers' way. She took the pail, about a third full of milk, and gripped it tightly between her thighs. With one hand she drew the calf's head into the bucket, forcing the muzzle into the milk. She had the other hand submerged in the milk and let Daisy suck her fingers. The little creature caught on quickly and soon the finger sucking wasn't necessary.

It was not a neat operation. Daisy would slurp, suck, and splash, pull her head out, and drool threads of milk about. And by an instinct designed to keep the newly freshened udder from caking and to stimulate the flow, she would butt furiously and wildly, making a great racket, slopping milk over Ann and giving her the souvenir of bruise-covered thighs until the weaning to grain was accomplished.

The milk, and its by-product of about three pounds of butter a week, was no more than we needed. We had three children to use it, and had to supply Virginia and her flow of paying guests. If there was anything left it went to the pigs.

My relations with Susan had become idyllic. She followed me like a lamb. I turned her out to one of my own pastures where, by arrangement, some young cattle of Paul's also were grazing. Coming out to the pasture gate at six-thirty in the morning, I would call out in what sounded like the recitative prelude to an operatic aria. "Here, Susaaaaaaaaaan!" Without fail, from some quarter of the pasture out of sight over the hill would come a long, answering "Moooooo!" She would meet me as I went in the direction of her call and follow me into the barn. I could count on this, morning and evening. It became one of the demonstrations to enthrall city-folk visitors and carry them off their feet with its bucolic appeal. "She is so gentle," I announced, "that I am not going to bother taking off those horns."

The sunrise scene in the pasture was a joy in itself. I would often find the last veils of mist lifting. They left behind a heavy-beaded dew such as I had never seen before. The pasture grasses and shrubs seemed gem-carpeted and festooned with pearls and diamonds. In bushes and fence corners the prize exhibits were crystalline circular webs with brilliant yellow and black spiders as gleaming spots of color at the center.

Milking became a pleasure beyond my expectations. Ann asked me what philosophic thoughts I entertained during the process as a result of bringing the supposed self-awareness of the so-called intellectual to the very fount of nature, or what Shaw called "man's foster mother."

None, I replied, describing the sensations of milking as chiefly a pleasantly warm vacuity. I must admit that is not wholly true, though partly so. The conscious feeling of "Here sit I, the city man" often suffused me with triumph and pride. The symbolic act of transition was accomplished. It detracted not a whit to reflect that ten-year-old Graham was quite as good a milker as I, and that Ann and even David were duly initiated in the art. This, I felt, as I listened to the ringing sound of the first jets upon the pail bottom give way to the foamy splashing—this is *basic*.

But by a process so gradual that I shrank from recognizing it, the idyll began to crumble. After a month or so, Susan no longer answered my calls. This dampened my burgeoning sentimentality but, I reasoned, why should I expect this to go on indefinitely? At first she was new. She was seeking identification, companionship, a sense of belonging. Now she is at home, at rest, in peace. Now she need no longer answer the call. It is enough that she comes.

Except that soon she stopped coming too. I had to go all the way after her and cajole or drive her in. But since there was no disciplined dairy herd to lead her, she was not easy to drive. When I went behind her to urge her along she would go—but in any old direction. It required either two people or a great deal of patient agility to get her into the barn.

I bought a halter. I would need it anyway, I reasoned, for it was late summer, the pasture was sparse, and I wanted to tether her out alone in the new alfalfa growth after the haying. So for several weeks I led her in and out, walking beside her, hand upon the halter.

After a period of success with that, she began to balk. She would stop and refuse to move. I would pull, plead, curse, and bellow at her in unseemly terms. By main strength I would drag her along a little stretch at a time, or else, by gymnastics, would hang onto the halter with one hand and reach back to swat her rump with the other. If I let go she would take off for the hills. I had run myself ragged across the pasture several times, chasing her.

My next recourse I considered a brilliant stratagem. She was tethered out to a drag log now. By leading her in and out at rope's end, I could play her like a game fish and be the equivalent of two handlers. I would lead her by the rope as long as she would follow. When she balked abruptly and stood her ground, I would pay out a little rope, double back, and flick her with it from the rear. She would try to rush off but I could curb and control her. This system convinced me that I had struck the solution. If she had been with a dairy herd, I reflected, this would never have happened. It was much like the problems with an only child.

But she developed a set of rodeo tricks. At the end of some ten feet of rope Susan would buck, dance, and kick up front and back, accompanied by a frenzied rolling of eyes and tossing of head. This was enough to drag me off my feet and leave me either scrambling to retrieve the rope or yanking profanely at it until Susan's outburst was subdued.

On a chilly night when I had brought Daisy from her customary stall into the main barn for greater warmth, I preceded Susan through the door with the lead rope. She got her forefeet and head inside, caught a glimpse of the unexpected presence, and took off like an escaped gas balloon. I gave her line as if playing a bass and checked her flight but could not make her re-enter. As a final expedient, I crawled through her stanchion myself, rope in hand, then braced my feet and warped her into her berth, inch by inch, by main strength. I began to feel that I would have to employ a windlass and set up a capstan in the middle of the barn.

On one frosty evening Susan went berserk in earnest. Several times she had tried to toss our young police dog, Ethan Allen. This I considered understandable. Now Susan lowered her head and made three considered efforts to get *me*. I sidestepped, larruped her, and gave her a drill-sergeant dressing-down.

When I had got Susan into the stanchion I said to Ann,

"It is not that I cannot control this perishing cow, but I'll be damned if I am going to let her carry weapons!" Gone was my sentimental notion that the horns could stay. We had heard disturbing suggestions that de-horning might dry her up. I phoned Dr. Miller. "Milk or no milk, come over here tomorrow and take off these horns."

During the night I searched my soul for traces of excessive timidity, or stupidity, in the management of that heifer which, I reflected bitterly, I had babied like my own daughter and given every good thing. How sharper than a serpent's tooth to have a thankless cow!

Searching the Scriptures is a long-standing habit with me in pursuit of many seemingly incongruous subjects. Something now lurked in dim remembrance. I tracked it down to Hosea 4:16: "For Israel slideth back as a backsliding heifer." "Thou too," I mumbled to myself, visualizing the prophet with an unruly cow-critter at rope's end, for from where but experience could such an inspired simile spring? The centuries have not altered the ways of the breed.

When Dr. Miller arrived with a heavy-set helper who had never appeared before, I poured into his patient ears a long defensive rehash of the case history. Like a wounded parent in a soap opera I cried, "What have I done wrong?"

Dr. Miller said placidly, "Oh, I reckon she was so quiet at first because she was run down and played out. After you got her fed up she began to feel her oats. Anyway, most farmers tell me that a cow with horns that starts acting up usually quiets right down when they're taken off. They know they have them. It just gets her to feeling playful."

"Playful!" I said bitterly.

"Well, that's how it starts. Then they discover what they can do, and begin to turn mean."

Years later, in Mexico, I visited the ranch of a breeder of brave bulls. In his small trial ring I saw them test the spirit of sharp-horned heifers, who can fight formidably, to determine which ones showed fighting qualities worth breeding.

Dr. Miller entered the barn with me and regarded Susan benevolently. "That's a pretty sharp pair of horns," he said cheerfully. "She could do a lot of damage."

"Will it dry her up altogether?" I asked.

"Probably not. Might fall off for a few days. The milk you lose won't be as important as having an accident."

He produced the ice-tong tie-up device and an enormous clipper like an oversized tree pruner, its lever power multiplied by gears. His accomplice, having tied Susan up, proceeded to twist her head.

"Don't mind if she blats, now," Dr. Miller said to me. "Sometimes they do, and then sometimes they don't make a sound."

He snapped his clippers. Susan emitted a short, sharp hoot like an old-fashioned plunger-operated klaxon. One horn flew through the air, clipped off a little below the skin. A quick twist of the head, another snip, another hoot, and the thing was done. I felt a pang of pity and terror.

"It doesn't hurt relatively any more than cutting your finger nail too close," Miller assured me. He proceeded to pinch the ends of the veins to check the slight bleeding, and packed the sockets with cotton. "Skin will form over these," he said. "I think she looks a lot better. They weren't good-looking horns." But to me she looked strange and somehow pitiful, with the two blobs of white cotton blooming absurdly where her weapons of defiance and aggression had been.

"Poor thing," Ann said, slightly depressed. "Maybe it doesn't hurt much, but it's against nature. It represents defeat."

And indeed, Susan appeared to know she was licked. She became docile as a lamb and remained so, with big questioning eyes and demure ways. Graham and I comforted her with apples for a few days, which set her to nuzzling our pockets hopefully whenever we appeared. The milk went down by half for two milkings. I fed her grain till it ran out her ears and brought her back to her everlasting eight quarts. Evidently, as with all large-souled people, her ordeal had turned her into a beautiful character.

CHAPTER SEVEN

Goin' Fishin'
or Gettin' Ready

LIKE ABE LINCOLN'S STORY of a wistful boy and gingerbread, there were few people who loved fishing more than I
did or got less of it than I did. From the earliest dawning of
the farm idea I had hoped that moving to Vermont would
bring me fishing opportunities. Then when we took the
Hand's Cove farm I felt certain that fishing would be a big
factor in our lives. As confidently as everybody said the well
was 250 feet deep, they also said the fishing was wonderful.

I was anxious to test this early. In the first days we saw a
steady traffic of cars and farm trucks driving in and parking
down by the blockhouse. Men would head off with fishlines
across the lower meadow and pasture toward the cove.

According to the mores, any man was free to cross his
neighbor's land to fish peaceably. Fishermen roved all over,
depending on the season and on where the fish were biting
best at the moment. I was prepared to honor this, but since
our farm had been unoccupied a long time, too great a variety

of people from near and far were infesting the place. A few days after we arrived someone made off with Meredith's tricycle, which she had left down by the blockhouse, where, of course, we weren't yet living. From that time I restricted fishing permission to near neighbors or villagers known to me. Other people I turned away firmly and in a few weeks the wholesale invasion ceased. But I was encouraged at the evidence that we inhabited a fisherman's Mecca.

David was my chief fellow enthusiast. Early on, he and I set out for the cove to study the prospects. Distances on the farm were surprising but the walks were grand. The road ended at the blockhouse. We went down across the meadow to the barbed-wire fence that divided it from the pasture; then across hummocky, grassy terrain to the light fringe of trees that lined the cove. Along the fences the lily-like dog-tooth violet, called yellow adder's-tongue thereabout, was abundant. So, too, were the gay white stars of bloodroot. Patches of true violets, both blue and white, dotted shady spots of the pasture. In damp places closer to the water the bright, joyous yellow of marsh marigold glowed in the spring green.

Where the rim of trees began the land sloped down sharply to the cove. This long arm of water curved back deeply into the woods. It was blue and clear, but near the mouth were great beds of high reeds with a broad channel winding through them to the main waters of the lake. Inward, at the shallowest parts, the cattails already grew, with arrowroot and what we discovered to be wild rice, which made the cove a choice stopover for migrant ducks. We had dreams of harvesting the wild rice for ourselves but the project was never realized. Across the cove on the south side was a scraggy wooded tangle that also was ours.

Later in the season a profusion of beautiful water lilies,

both yellow and white, moved into the shallower water, and small frogs sat on their leaves in the classic image. A basso-profundo croak sounded intermittently. An 1837 letter from one of the Hands spoke jokingly of "reverence for the lonely spot near the Bull Frog's Nest"—presumably meaning the farm—but I felt this was its inspiration.

Mud turtles basked at the edges. By August the greater part of the cove grew shallow, for Champlain, a slowly diminishing lake for all its vastness, often recedes as much as twenty feet or more from its southern shorelines. This summertime receding of the water, plus the heavy winter freeze and subsequent violent breakup, made a permanent dock impossible, even on the shoreline north of the cove. In the late summer all but the deepest channels of the cove were overgrown, and fishing was transferred wholly to the lake until winter cleared and replenished the cove waters again.

Now, in April, as we stepped down through the trees from the pasture level to the partly grassy, partly muddy cove shore, a marvelous isolation enveloped us. All else seemed curtained off, shut away behind us. Exposed roots from the near trees writhed and twisted everywhere, some arching up from the soil to trip the unwatchful. This was from the trampling of cattle coming to the water's edge to drink. An occasional fallen tree trunk offered a seat to the lazy.

The sun poured down on this quiet, sheltered world. The water was still and glistening. It rippled gently from the slightest stir of air and the reeds took up the motion exaggeratedly. It was a composition in light and shadow, gold, green, and blue. In this place one could spend hours. It had healing and restorative qualities.

Birds were the conspicuous life. Redwing blackbirds were the dominant population, though woodpeckers, kingfishers, and hawks were often seen. The blue heron and white egret were spotted with fair frequency, and there was a lone, solitary eagle whom we saw from time to time, mostly describing vast, high circles above us, but occasionally dipping to some hidden eyrie in the woods across the cove. But the chief impressions were the melodious notes and flashing spots of color of the myriad busy redwings among the reeds.

Stacks of small, short logs here and there perplexed us. We learned later that these were floats to which muskrat traps were fastened. The creatures abounded. Their runs could be seen at many points along the edge and some of their tunnels were visible in the banks. I am neither trapper nor hunter, but each year we leased the rights to trap muskrats and to build duck blinds in the appropriate seasons.

On this exploratory visit David and I saw at once that we were not alone; indeed, we seldom were by ourselves in the cove in the early fishing season. An old man was hunkered down at the water's edge. He was keeping an eye on several lines that disappeared into the water. In the soft ground he had poked some flexible green sticks, and into each of these one of his lines was notched. As we stood there one stick was jerked violently. The fisherman sprang up and began pulling in, hand over hand. With a rushing splash and flurry at the last, in shallow water, he drew up a fat striped yellow perch.

When he had unhooked him and tossed him into a pail he rebaited the hook. I saw there were several hooks on the line, in the last two feet or so, while at the very end was a heavy weight. He took the line about three feet from the weight, spun it in a rapid circle like a lasso, and let it fly. It soared well out and down with a splash, the line playing out smoothly from where he had let it fall as he hauled in.

We approached now, saying "Hello," and the old man

said, "How do." We made mutual introductions. His name was Tommy and he lived up behind one of the nearby apple orchards. As time went on we knew him well in a variety of functions.

Looking at the rods we carried, he said, "That ain't rightly what you want, except you're in a boat. Bamboo pole an' a float'll do, but best thing here in the cove is a plain ol' heave line like I'm usin'. It'll get ya plenty of whatever's bitin'."

"How are you doing?"

He contemplated his lines and the still, blue water deliberately. "Well, they ain't bitin' very rank today."

I looked in the pail. In a half-bucket of water were at least three perch and a couple of other fish.

"Perch and punkinseeds," Tommy said. The latter was the local name for sunfish, chiefly bluegills.

Tommy became one of our several mentors on fishing matters. Basically a shiftless old man, he epitomized the proverbial character who is always either goin' fishin' or gettin' ready. From him we began to learn the catalogue of fish in our waters, though our knowledge of and direct encounter with these numerous kinds was acquired over a month or more.

There were the prolific perch and punkinseeds. The ubiquitous catfish was on hand, and with him a cousin, distinguished only by the shape of the tail and running smaller, called locally a bullhead or bullpout and prized by many well above the perch for sweetness of flesh.

The burbot, called a ling locally, was a big fresh-water cod. Like the large, whitish, and much too numerous sheepshead, it was held in low repute and generally thrown back. There were carp, also, among the scorned fish.

A popular fish often running to good size was known triply as a crappie, strawberry bass, or rock bass. The aristocrats of these waters, common enough to be accessible but aloof enough to make their catching an event, were the small-mouth black bass, the great northern pike, and the walleyed pike. All of these dwelt in the main lake and landing any of them was an occasion for celebration.

Both species of pike could be caught in the summer—and we got them. Yet the best time for them, and the season for getting the giants among them, was the dead of winter, fishing through the ice.

David and I got a hint of what the lake held, about two weeks after we arrived. We were simply taking a walk along the wooded shore north of the point. Looking directly down into several feet of clear water, we were suddenly hushed with astonishment to see a shadowy form glide out of the deeper water and lazily pass beneath us. He was a great northern pike, looking to us like a submarine, perhaps five feet long, with a slender, savage jaw. In a moment, before we could catch our breath, he flicked his tail and veered back into the opaque deeper water. It was conventional to bewail that we had no tackle with us. We owned nothing that could hold the like of him and we never knew of one of such proportions caught in summer. This was not the only such sighting. More than a year later Graham and I, coming along the wooded shore after a storm, saw a whole school of pike in a great range of sizes.

After our encounter with Tommy in the cove I bought heave lines for us, ganged three or four hooks on them as instructed, and mastered the art of tossing them out. There is no easier or lazier form of fishing and we got some nice messes of pan fish that way. The chief point of caution was to make certain one end was anchored. Once I heaved out the entire line, which was swallowed up in the cove.

We also made an expedition, on advice, to a dirt-road village called Whiting, where, in a frantically cluttered general store, we bought several long yellow bamboo poles, to rig up lines with a float or bobber. These we used mainly on rare extraterritorial fishing jaunts, generally with farm hands, to a meandering, much-fished creek engagingly named the Lemon Fair, which seemed to tote up five miles of sinuosity to every two of linear progress. In the spring thaw the simple Lemon Fair flooded miles of fields and roads.

Promptly I bought a rowboat, brand new, for forty dollars, made by a local man—the same whom Ann had caught surreptitiously peeping in the cistern to see how we were fixed for water. I was not a casting fisherman, which barred me at once from the élite. I was the sort of person who would attempt a cast and find himself with a reel so bunched with line that it looked like cotton candy. Since then I have mastered what some regard as a lesser form of casting—with a spinner.

The boat gave us our true piscatorial excitements. We were so impatient to use our new boat that we hadn't given it enough of the necessary soaking to close its seams completely, so David and I took turns bailing. In the channel through the reeds I hooked a seven-pound catfish. This monstrous, ugly brute remains the largest fish I've ever caught. In any previous phase of our lives we would have disdained it. Under the new regimen, with our vision of living off the land, we were determined to have it for dinner. Skinned—a rough job; I'll take scaling any time—it proved to be delicate and delicious —a bountiful meal for six.

Half the pleasure of this game was that we seldom failed to catch something, and with that satisfying hard tug at the end of the line you never knew what was coming up. Once it was a big eel, also a good dish. The bad days were when the wind was blowing hardest—it was always blowing some. Then the

clay would color the water and the old-timers like Tommy or
Mr. Gregoire would cast an eye at the choppy, murky water
and say, "It's too roily."

One Sunday afternoon David and I were drifting along the
rock ledges along our northern shore. I was trolling for pike
with an elaborate spoon rig called a Lake Champlain special.
David, on the stern seat, was using a little old rod and a
worm.

He felt a big strike, and then his line went limp. After a
few moments he began to reel it in to check his bait, when
abruptly a big fish leaped right behind him, on his line. By
sheer reflex he yanked it in over the seat. Then we both began to shriek and the fish began to fight, jumping so that we
feared it would go over the side.

Every known rule for landing a game fish had been vio-
lated. I got my foot on it, then a good handgrip, and wrapped
it in the folds of my landing net. It was secure—a northern
pike, nineteen inches long. I pried open the mouth gingerly,
for pike have razor-sharp teeth at the sides. It proved to be
hooked extremely lightly through the membrane of the roof
of the mouth. The fish had been pulled in by sheer mutual
surprise. The hook would never have withstood a rush if that
pike had been played conventionally, and its teeth would
have cut David's line, for he was not rigged with a metal snell;
we made sure of that thereafter.

David was so ecstatic as to practically float in air above the
boat. He trembled violently for twenty minutes, teeth chat-
tering, then compounded his triumph by catching a big
sheepshead. He had carried off the honors at six years old.
Before we ate that pike, in a state feast on Monday night,
David was photographed holding his prize. I was happier that
he had got it than if I had got it myself—slightlier.

My own afternoon of triumph was in a context faintly embarrassing. With the coming and going of Virginia's customers through the summer, fishing was an attraction to many—some of whom were our friends, and some, strangers. It often fell to me to be guide and oarsman. In one such case, four adults and David were in the boat. We were using live minnows in quest of black bass off the ledges.

There were five lines in the water from one small boat. I got a quick strike, and after a dramatic struggle with a high-leaping fish, netted a three-pound bass, seventeen and a half inches long. Everyone's eagerness was whetted—all bait was checked, the minnows exhorted to shut up and keep swimming. Five minutes later I had a two-pound bass. Envious quips were made about my having the best seat. There was enough edge to them that, though it was a silly maneuver, I made the symbolic gesture of changing seats and fishing off the other side. In five more minutes I had a one-pound bass. Nothing else was caught that day, no one else landing anything better than his own live bait.

An adjunct to the fishing was the art and craft of night-crawler gathering. These great fat worms, replaced in this effete latter day by polyethylene fakes, I was taught to collect by the plumber, Gregoire.

On a wet spring night you could get them by the quart by prowling around garden beds or any loose soil with a flashlight. When they were flat out on the ground they were helpless—but when only part way out of their holes, they could retract with astonishing speed for such sluggish creatures, and the lightning snatch was essential. Sometimes there was a tug of war that left me feeling like a chagrined robin, with half a worm. It was a curiously fascinating nocturnal sport.

The further refinement into which I was inducted was

night-crawler ranching, on the ever-normal granary principle. Leave nothing to chance. Run no hazard of a wormless drought.

The captive crawlers were kept in a bushel basket of dirt in the cellar, where they would keep even through the winter and breed. The most striking and symbolically fitting fact was that the favorite food on which night crawlers fatten and breed forever is coffee grounds. It seemed like an obscure link with the lost life of the city and night crawlers of another breed.

CHAPTER EIGHT

Barber, Barber, Shave a Pig

WE ACQUIRED THREE PIGS early in the first summer, buying them from a French-Canadian farmer named Aunchman—an onomatopoeic name for a pig farmer. I always thought of him as *the* Aunchman because his name suggested to me the title of some primitive tribal dignitary, or else a character in a Thomas Hardy novel, like the Reddleman. His landsmen pronounced the name Haunchman, for the way of French Canadians with an "h" is much like that of a Cockney.

The piglets were Chester whites, about a foot long but a yard loud. It was our first lesson in the odd skill of cornering a small and frantic pig and snatching him up by the hind legs. The sounds reminded me of the version of "Rumpelstiltskin" that I knew as a child. When the dwarf had the disappointment of hearing his true name pronounced the book said, "He shruck awful." That came instantly to mind with the appalling outcries of the terrified shoats. Clamoring and kicking, they were dropped one by one into a grain sack, and the furiously wriggling, squealing bundle was put in our car.

Two of the pigs were castrated males, destined to be pork. The other was a sow. A policy was established and firmly followed. The pigs for slaughter were left nameless. The one we looked to for future prolific farrowing was called Sowzy.

We had a hog house and pen in tolerable shape. The interior had a cracked, slightly tilted cement floor and big cement feeding troughs which were not easy to clean. Graham daubed on the door, with white paint: "Piggery—Beware."

The outside pen had been set up, before our time, as a chicken run. Chicken wire is no kind of fencing for pigs— even young ones. I tried to get away with it for a while. Our whole history with pigs was marked by a progressive boarding-up, and otherwise reinforcing, of the hog-pen fence. Generally, though, with all we were trying to do, plus my natural procrastination, spurts of this fence work chiefly followed jail breaks.

Every so often, as they grew, the pigs would root or wriggle an escape hatch and turn up on the lawn, wreaking terrible havoc around shrubs and some young trees we had planted, or else would be seen in the pasture, or vanishing up the road. Then the cry would go up: "The pigs are out!" and all within earshot would mobilize for action.

Graham and David were stout swineherds, though given to stirring up the choral ensemble in such roundups. It is hard to sell a boy on the stratagem of quietly and slowly closing in.

One time in the autumn, when the pigs had attained to a substantial size, Ann happened out onto the lawn just in time to see the three white blobs nearing the crest of the hill on the road up to the brick house. Meredith, now almost three years old, was at the top of the hill, clad in a red cloak with peaked hood that we called the Dalai Lama outfit.

I came out and heard Ann shouting, "Meredith! *Mer-edith!* Stop the pigs!"

As was her way even then—and still is—Meredith leaped into the breach. She started to charge down the hill, a tiny red-cloaked figure like a baby Fury, arms outflung as if to gather in the world, shrilling a fearsome "*Yaaaayyyyyyyy!*"

The pigs were appalled. They stopped in their tracks, wheeled, and tore madly downhill toward home and refuge, the midget avenger hard on their heels. The Gadarene swine could not have been more frightened of their demons.

There is much misapprehension about pigs and they are often libelled. They are called dirty, when, in fact, they are far more fastidious than cattle and unlike them do not willingly lie in their own excrement. A dirty pig is a pig kept in dirt in cramped quarters with no escape from it. It is just fate that the odor of pig manure is far worse than that of cows or horses—that of humans, often used as fertilizer in some parts of the world, is worse yet. A pig allowed to graze on range and select his lying-down place will keep himself immaculate. He will wallow in mud or water in hot weather because he has no pores to help cool him.

A pig is smart; even a stupid one is full forty times brighter than a cow of high IQ and can vie creditably with some people—especially a few who lead their lives among pigs. Also, given a chance, a pig is amiable and affectionate.

Their one deserved piece of bad billing relates to their gluttony. That cannot be talked away. They rush to be fattened for the kill. Their manners are deplorable. In contrast to the placid, ruminative eating habits of the cow, the pig slurps, gobbles, grunts, crawls into the trough, shoves away his mates, and will knock you off your feet in the rush when you come into the pen with the slop pail.

In the late fall, after the diet of milk swill and pork builder had been capped, for the two porkers, by lavish rations of cornmeal, the season of the knife was at hand. I approached the slaughter as a challenge. Like most city men I had no experience whatever of gutting and butchering. Bloodless and clean meat was all I knew. Yet as a fisherman I had gutted fish and saw no reason not to look on the pigs as though they were bigger, warm-blooded fish. I felt an obligation of honor to learn something of the skill. I could yield to no squeamishness, holding it contemptible to eat meat if I could not face up to the obtaining of that meat when it was logical for me to do so in my new life.

Tommy, our sometime fishing companion and wood hauler, agreed to slaughter for me while I served as apprentice. Tommy had a small farm but didn't farm it. He was a putterer who fished and drifted through various forms of casual, seasonal oddments of work. He was always the man you might get to do something if you could find him. His wife, Resi, I presume from Thérèse, worked somewhat more steadily.

When Ann asked Tommy if he could butcher he said, "Oh yes, my father learned me bootcherin' an' all that, so's I wouldn't get run off." He had not got run off but his little inherited farm had got run down. He had a mournful team of horses, seldom used, that he simply turned loose to forage over a good bit of area, summer and winter. Those horses could turn up anywhere in a radius of miles. This used to distress us in seasons of slim pickins, as when the snow was deep. But when I asked Tommy once, in the heavy snows, how his horses would get anything to eat he said cheerfully, "Oh, they'll make a livin'."

He hauled in some stove wood for me once, on a sharing

basis. We included in the load some rotting beams from a dismantled building. They had been dumped in a gully long ago. Parts of them were all right as summer wood, for a chunk stove. As we loaded one of those battered beams onto the truck I said, "It's pretty rotten, isn't it?" Tommy said, as I heard him say of many things afterward, "Well, it won't get no better." He was the New England equivalent of what the Southerner would call "no 'count."

Butchering day, in late November, had a dreary overcast and a damp, biting wind. Tommy came down in the morning with a .22-caliber pistol. The hogs knew something was up the instant we entered the pen. I don't know by what processes of divination, but a special terror came over them. Possibly it was a sense of our purposefulness. When Tommy raised the pistol to draw a bead the pigs began to charge wildly around the interior of the hog house.

Finally we cornered one; he stood with forefeet spread, head slightly lowered. Tommy knelt a few feet away, and aimed between the eyes. With the light snap of the pistol the pig gave a little shriek and a start but stood his ground. The bullet was somewhere in that thick skull. Tommy fired again. The pig gave a snort, his front legs buckled, and the long heavy body dropped sideways. With a swift move Tommy was beside the head, a sharp knife slashing into the throat. There was a dark gush.

"Got to get 'em quick," he said, breathing hard from the exertion. "That's the trouble, shootin'em. Times you don't get 'em quick, they won't bleed."

Pistol in hand again, he stalked the other victim, got him with one shot, and brandished the knife. While this ritual went on, Sowzy put aside her anxieties and began to browse eagerly at the slit throat of her first-deceased brother.

Tommy had a pair of hay hooks with him, the same cruel hooks longshoremen use. He snagged a dead pig in the mouth with one and dragged it to the door of the building. I followed suit with the other. They were not tremendous hogs, but of a good size for lean pork—a little over two hundred pounds. They were not easy to drag.

Picking them up by the feet, we heaved them onto Tommy's old truck. The rest of the work was to be done at his place, for he had the equipment there.

Tommy's ramshackle, paint-peeled little house sat amidst its few acres on a high knoll. Orchards flanked it on two sides. But the house and the area behind it where we worked looked out over the heads of the orchard trees, down the falling slopes to the lake, and across to the Adirondack ranges. The mountains were purple against dark gray, their subtle contours lost. The cloud ceiling was low. The wind was nagging and spit in our faces now and then with spattering raindrops.

Near the house was a shed with crossbars, where we would hang the pigs in due course. In front of this we pushed them off the truck and they fell with a fleshy thwack. Here Tommy had rigged his barrel for scalding. It was a big hogshead, which he had heeled deep into the ground, on a slope, so that its lower lip was just a few inches above ground level. It was at a sixty- to seventy-degree angle.

Well behind the house, on a broad expanse of bare ground beside a plowed place, Tommy was kindling a huge fire. Almost entirely hemmed in by the fire, but with one narrow wedge of approach to it, was a huge, cracked but watertight black iron kettle. It had probably seen use as a potash kettle, and perhaps as a sugaring kettle, too.

The old beams, stumps, and wind-fallen limbs that I had

gathered and shared with Tommy previously were the staple fuel, but there was also a heap of battered, threadbare, and blown-out tires.

"Nothin' burns hotter," Tommy said, and with his wood base blazing, flung on some tires, cocking a couple up against the sides of the kettle.

I knew in a general way that this was true but I'd never before seen the furious, hissing flame with which they burned. The whole great pyre, the entire kettle, was wreathed and lapped with deep-orange flames. Black billows of the fetid, rubbery smoke swirled about us erratically. We could find no fixed position windward of it in the persistent, crazy gale. This demoniacal orgy of wind, flame, and smoke disturbed me a little. The bloodletting and now this scene out of *Macbeth* made me feel caught in a reversion to barbarism. Tommy was tranquil. He puttered around, or squatted on his heels, or threw on fuel, patiently. I let my own gaze roam from the witches' cauldron to the lake and distant mountains, to the orchards, fields, and farmhouses dotted about. I stood in the wind, the stink, and the roar, with rain flicking at me, wondering vaguely how I had got there.

The water in the huge pot was at the humming simmer of rising bubbles.

"Isn't it hot enough?" I asked.

"Got to have a good rollin' boil," Tommy explained. "You dip 'em, and it ain't hot enough, and you just set the bristles."

The water began to seethe more. There were a few tires left.

"You can throw on another tire," Tommy said.

I hesitated, with a deep-rooted magpie chinchiness that I have about using up junk. I am a hoarder from way back.

"We don't need them, do we? You may want them some other time."

"You can throw 'em on," Tommy assured me, with the blithe freedom of using that was his philosophy. "I don't care for 'em." He was not laying up worn tires on this earth for moth and rust to corrupt. I threw on another.

The deep rolling boil began soon, and with it, the action. Tommy kicked away some burning logs that had enveloped the approach to the kettle. With two buckets apiece we dipped into the boiling vat and rushed to dump the water into the hogshead. I guess we filled it about halfway, considering its angle, and I sloshed my shins amply with scalding water in the process.

Working together, we drew up one of the pigs by the great hook in its mouth, and grunting with exertion, shoved it in, rear first, and dunked it up and down, *slop slop*, in the scalding, steaming bath, splashing ourselves some more in the bargain. After four or five immersions we drew it out. Tommy deftly removed the hook from the jaws and thrust it through the tendons of the hind legs, drawn together. Then we repeated the dipping, head first.

"Well," Tommy said, "I hope it was hot enough. I hope they ain't set."

The wet steaming carcass lay at our feet with a drowned look. Tommy went off in a hurry to kindle up the fire again and refill the depleted cauldron. I took up a scraper and went to work.

A hog scraper is shaped like half an orange, with a handle in the center of the convex side. Thus it has a circular edge. You simply scrape away, tediously, persistently. The water had been hot enough, the coarse white hair came away readily, in soggy masses, along sides and back and belly. It was much harder in creases and joints, and on the legs and head.

I was wondering what to do about these difficult spots when Tommy came back. He took from a case two old-fashioned straight razors and handed one to me. We settled to the slower, meticulous work of clean-shaving head, joints, legs, and any obstinate patches on the body.

When we had finished we began the whole process again with the second pig. As we came to the shaving stage a station wagon with a Massachusetts license pulled up in the road, and a man got out and approached us. Both Tommy and I stood up, expectantly. I thought it quite possible that it was someone looking for me.

The man cast an eye from one to the other of us with a cagey, suspicious expression. He glanced from the run-down house to Tommy, associated them, and addressed him. "You got any antiques, any furniture, china or anything you want to sell?"

Tommy ran his hand over his head and hitched up his pants, which were wet and sagging—as were mine, clinging coldly to flesh in the wind. "Well," he said, "you can come in an' look."

I had never seen an antique cruiser at work in the back country. As they disappeared I ruminated over it but knelt down with my razor to my tonsorial chores.

The thing that had shocked me about this operation was that the clear, soft though tight white skin seemed completely human. It was like the clean-shaven cheek of a young, healthy lad who hasn't been shaving long. Abruptly, something familiar came to me. Again and again I had been startled, even in our limited adventure, to come upon an actual agrarian root of some classic of nonsense, nursery rhyme, or proverb. Here, I felt, flourishing my razor deftly about an ear, was the origin of "Barber, barber, shave a pig."

After about fifteen minutes Tommy and the stranger appeared again and I watched them go back and forth. They took six straight spindle-back chairs out to the station wagon. I could see that the finish was poor but the shape good. The man also emerged with a small pile of dishes, which he stowed in carefully. At last he handed over something to Tommy, then he drove away.

Tommy came back. He worked for a few minutes.

"That feller was givin' good money," he said finally.

I could see that he was satisfied that he had "took" him to a reasonable degree.

"Resi'll kill me when she sees I've sold them chairs. She was pretty choice of 'em. But that feller give me twenty dollars for the chairs an' five for the dishes."

That was Tommy the philosopher in operation. Whatever the chairs and china may have been, he didn't care for them any more than for the old tires. Selling was what the furniture and china proved to be good for, as the tires were good for burning. How many times before had stuff left the house that way? I felt chiefly a rush of pity for Resi, who was "pretty choice of 'em," and the shock that waited her return. For Tommy—he could always replace a chair with an orange crate.

He stood up. A dilapidated cat that Tommy seemed to have worn out, too, wandered from behind the shed, rubbed sensuously along the back of a scraped pig, uttered a terse comment, then fell to sniffing delicately at the pink slashed throat, the edges of which were slightly curled outward and whitened from the scalding.

Tommy contemplated it with high geniality. "Hello, kitty," he said. "You want some guts?"

We went back to work. The rest was a dogged matter of hoisting the pigs up by their hind legs and gutting them. As I had reasoned, it was not essentially different from gutting a fish, except bigger. It was like cleaning a small whale. The optimistic cat and a party of friends rallied round.

Our deal with Tommy was five dollars and the heads, for, alas, I am too finicky for the delicacies called shouse meat and headcheese. Late that afternoon, with the white, dismembered pigs stowed in the back of the car, feeling faintly like ax murderers, Ann and I took our first pork to the Middlebury locker.

It was December 1, the same day eight heifers were brought down to board in our barn to help keep the calves warm—but that's another story.

CHAPTER NINE

Steam-Heated Calves

DAISY WAS THE ENTERING WEDGE. She should not have been kept; her proper function had been getting herself born so that Susan would give milk. Sentimentality prevailed—we were doomed from the time of that bucolic, Keatsian, Grecian-urn procession through green pastures when we led back to our barn "that heifer lowing at the skies" the morning of Daisy's birth.

Against all original designs we let ourselves get caught in the cattle trap. The steps of involvement went about like this: we would keep Daisy because she was so appealing. Someday we might sell her as a freshening heifer. In our big drafty old barn we needed more livestock to keep it warm enough for Susan, so we were going to board a dozen or more head of yearling heifers of our neighbors. Since we would have them there, we might as well cope with a few more creatures of our own. We had become interested in the idea of purebred Jerseys; an opportunity arose for us to acquire a couple of heifer calves, ergo . . .

Don't look for solid logic in that, for it isn't there. I did not come squarely to grips with the time projections in all this, or with the fact that the slow increase in milking stock would produce far more milk than we could use (Susan alone did that, the superflux fattening the pigs and chickens), yet far less milk than would make an economic operation proportionate to the time consumed.

The printer, Ira Payne, was a leading breeder of Jerseys. The likes of us could not afford anything that might be for sale from his lordly herd near Albany. Yet he informed us that he could get us two purebred heifer calves of an age with Daisy from the herd of a friend of his. Raised to yearlings, and bred, even these would have been too costly for us, but for some reason or other the man's herd was at peak and he would let these go quite cheaply. Mr. Payne assured us that they were a sound buy and generously said that he himself would fetch them to us in a truck of his own. We bought.

On the sixth of November, Payne arrived in a small cattle truck with the calves and their documents. We got them unloaded and into the pen I had originally built for Daisy, and which I had reinforced.

We were quite carried away. They were the same size as Daisy but far more delicately modeled, and sensitive. Intensely alert and perky, they were most winsome. Again, the fatal pet psychology rather than hard-fisted cattle husbandry prevailed. One was a light, pale tan in color; the other, markedly darker, had a reddish cast.

After giving us a bit of counsel, Mr. Payne departed and we pursued the process of making friends with the calves. Both had registered names, which we did not intend to use except for record. The lighter we called Taffy; the darker, Handy—from Hand's Cove.

The next day we put Daisy with them—the peasant's child playing with the aristocrat's children. Their care seemed simple enough but, like all else to do with creatures, unceasing. They were grained in a feed trough, a bucket of water was boxed into a corner, and a thick bedding of oat straw was laid down for them. This was the tough part; it had to be freshened up daily, and every couple of days, as it grew damp and packed, the whole load, heavy with urine and manure, had to be forked over the side of their pen and shoveled out of the barn. Then the bedding had to be renewed completely.

This routine worked out nicely during the brief remaining time of warm Indian summer. Then ensued the colder, misty-moisty weather. The barn grew bleakly chilly. I went up to Paul's and pressed him firmly about bringing down the yearling Holsteins he was to board with us. The next day he and I together herded down eight head—I had hoped for more—and maneuvered them into the row of stanchions on the north aisle, opposite Susan and the calves. The steamy breath of these lumbering, oafish creatures was the promise to me of the animal warmth so vitally needed.

As December advanced, signs greeted us that at first we mistook for beauty rather than trouble. We called to each other and gazed in admiration the first time we saw a snow squall move off the Adirondacks and approach us across the lake in a folded white curtain until we were enveloped in its silent swirls. David and Meredith were gleeful—he was home from school with "the itch," an impetigo or some other mysterious outbreak. At last, the next morning, we saw the distinct snow line appear on the heights of the Adirondacks, west, and Green Mountains, east. It lay along their crests but would creep down and down in ensuing weeks until white rose from the valleys to meet it. The weather was growing really cold. In the evenings we would set chestnuts to roast on top of the coal stove, which by now was fired-up in our living room.

On the nineteenth, Daisy refused grain. It became a day of mingled harassments: light, sifting snow; the battery in my car had frozen and burst; our sow in heat had to be shipped off for breeding. Dr. Miller came to see about Daisy. Too cold in the barn, he said, but doctored her. I began a series of phone calls to see if more heifers could be found to board; Paul's eight and our little band just didn't generate heat enough—not for young calves, anyway. A man promised me four but he never came through with them.

Per instruction, I began taking the calves warm water to drink—we couldn't leave water for them any more, as it froze solid. I freshened their bedding daily and piled it deep. Yet two days later Handy was sick and Dr. Miller was summoned again.

He could not come until late in the day, but we realized that heroic measures were called for. Ann, Virginia, and I took counsel and decided that one way or another the calves must be got out of the drafty, cold barn.

The only tight place outside the houses proper that we could possibly turn to this use was the small, one-room building behind my granary study. It served as an auxiliary bedroom, for it was a finished clapboarded structure, with proper curtained window, electricity, and hardwood floor. If we used it now there was no doubt it would be damaged; there was also no doubt that if we didn't our calves would perish, whereas even if we did there was no certainty they would survive.

We acted: took the bed out, and the chair; took down the curtains. But there was no heat. For this, as a temporary expedient, I got out the old portable kerosene stove. We used it seldom but it was always indispensable when we resorted to it.

Kerosene fires, calves, and thick straw bedding are a bad combination. The little room wasn't more than ten by five. I penned off one end of it with a partition held in place by stout hook-and-eye fasteners. We tacked down tarred roofing paper to try to protect the floor a little, and strewed heavy bedding over that. We brought the calves up one at a time— a long, cold, hard trek from the barn. Then I lit up the kerosene stove on the safe side of the barrier.

This was not a satisfactory heat solution. The stove could not be run long in an unvented room without killing off the calves by carbon monoxide. Turning it off and on made wide temperature variations and would be an insuperable problem at night. As soon as the transfer had been made, I drove to Middlebury and came back with a portable electric steam radiator. This required filling and checking of valves, and in action it simmered and bubbled away like a pot of stew, but it gave sufficient heat and was no fire hazard. Its limitations as a heater were an advantage, if anything, for though some heat was essential we also had to guard against too much.

By the time this de luxe flat in a fine residential neighborhood was tenanted and operable, Dr. Miller arrived. Amazement is too weak a word; he was, at the least, dumfounded. He agreed, when speech was vouchsafed him again by the kindly gods, that some such measures were the only hope.

All three calves had severe bloody diarrhea and ominous temperatures. They staggered about on their weak legs and made an appalling mess and stench, which required continual cleaning up and renewal of bedding. Dr. Miller diagnosed hemorrhagic septicemia, shook his head over the matter, medicated, and departed.

The next morning they were still alive and up, though wobbly. This was December 22. We coddled, cosseted, and cajoled the calves through the Christmas season. When cleaned up, they formed an appropriately intimate and appealing manger scene. They mended slowly, with one frightening day's relapse.

The news of this *tour de force* spread through the town with telepathic speed. It was the most famous thing we ever did in Vermont. There came a procession of sightseers. Every farmer, neighbor, or acquaintance who could muster the nerve trooped down to see for himself this prodigy of steam-heated calves on a hardwood floor. I am sure it is talked of yet. It fitted every preconception of the mad city folk. It brought jokes and loud laughter, but at the same time, I believe, some grudging admiration for sheer determination and invention.

The calves should not have survived; it was the next thing to positively illegal for them to do so, considering the history. But survive they did. In the meantime we had our first farm Christmas, at sub-zero temperatures that Susan and the heifers withstood, but which would have finished off the calves.

Each house had a Christmas tree, which the boys and I had cut in our own woods. We dined on our own chickens and ducks, raised by Virginia, slaughtered by me, plucked and prepared by Virginia and Ann. The chicken-plucking Ann remembers as an ordeal of stench and sore fingers. Many foods smell delicious when they reach the table that have had a woeful stink in their primal stages of preparation. The chickens, dipped in scalding water to loosen the feathers, as Tommy and I dunked the pigs, were an offense to the nostrils.

Yet the Christmas season was a joy to us. Meredith was just at the age to relish its full impact, and until she collapsed into tears from the sheer abundance of it all, as children often do, she exclaimed over each gift she received, "Oh—I needed that *terribly!*"

By the end of the holidays the calf crisis was over. The fearful sick-bay cleanup had given way to a normal operation, though it was always cumbersome, for the straw and manure could not sit in the back yard and had to be carted off in a wheelbarrow.

The calves inhabited their select studio apartment, or as the British would call it, bed-sitter, through the winter. Once they were well again they generated enough heat for themselves in the small tight room, during all except the most rigorous cold spells, when their radiator had to be plugged in as a precaution. With spring, they went back down to the barn.

They had been the kind of tenants after whom refinishing is unavoidable. The floor was stained and dented a little, though not nearly as badly as it would have been if we hadn't been diligent. The wallboard was stained and scuffed, requiring to be scrubbed down and painted. The room was never used again in so unconventional a fashion but it always had, for us, a special associative aura, like a place that was an emergency hospital in a city with the plague.

CHAPTER TEN

Sowzy

YOU MAY RECALL that the pig, Sowzy, was the only one of the three permitted the dignity of a name because we did not wish to be on intimate terms with our sausage and pork chops. For Sowzy we had in mind the noble calling of farrowing sow. When her brothers had departed this life under the ruthless hands of Tommy and myself, Sowzy inhabited the piggery in luxurious solitude, enjoying a monopoly of the abundant food scraps of a family whose children were poor eaters.

The only trouble was, she kept getting out. I had never got around to a reconstruction of the chicken-wire portions of the pig run, but had kept adding miscellaneous planks along its sides, higher and higher, by improvisation—one of the symptoms of my ultimate incapacity to cope with the farm. Whenever her mind was set upon it seriously Sowzy, with her wit and her weight, could contrive to get out.

As the chill autumn weather advanced she was bound to be kept indoors more and more. Even before the calf crisis beset us Ann prophetically took a dubious view, contending that the piggery was damp and its cement floor cold. We kept it bedded thick with straw, and at such times as Sowzy was indoors there was no escape problem.

In the course of her numerous jail breaks, Sowzy managed to turn herself into something of a pet. We had not imagined that she had such affectionate and sociable propensities. Sometimes we allowed her to putter around between the house and the piggery, though at hazard that the besetting demon of swine would prompt her to root up our nut trees or shrubs. Often, as we went back and forth, up and down hill between the houses, Sowzy would tag along at our heels, grunting and whiffling, from time to time nudging our shins amiably. She often went with me to my office and poked about the yard until I went back.

When Graham or I went far down into the meadows to fetch the cows who were being allowed to graze on some scattered late growth, Sowzy would follow on the entire, long trek, snorting to and fro, investigating things in a small orbit, but always keeping up with the company and returning to the house with us again exactly like a dog. She trailed Meredith and David around with equal persistence. As the children played games she would stand about with a quizzical snout, longing to be included. After her kind, Sowzy was both warm-hearted and intelligent.

It was sometime in December that I had a professional guest at the farm for a matter of four or five days. Part of my work was to serve as an editorial trouble-shooter and consultant to publishers, authors, and agents. The religious department of a publishing house had sent me a manuscript by a liberal Baptist clergyman of the Midwest, whom I'll call Dr. J. C. Loft. As an outgrowth of my recommendations, it was arranged that Dr. Loft would come to the farm and spend a few days working over the manuscript with me to get it in final shape for publication.

Dr. Loft was an interesting and genial man, although he seemed to us to have more of the personality of a traveler in the wholesale furniture business than of a man of the cloth. He was small, lean, weathered; he smoked big cigars and talked rapidly.

On the second evening of his stay at the farm, we were seated in the living room of the blockhouse discussing theological matters. Ann, who always takes a lively part in whatever I have on the fire, was with us. The children were all asleep.

Dr. Loft paused in the midst of a remark, held up his cigar like an antenna, and said, "Don't I hear something outside?"

Indeed he did: a muffled but distinct thump, thump, rustle, rustle, scurry. I went outside and stood on the doorstep, peering around. Everything was quiet. I went to the barn and saw that all the cow-critters were where they belonged.

Back in the living room we settled down to theology again. After a while a fresh outburst of thumping, scurrying, and scrabbling was heard. This time it was accompanied by loud whifflings and snortings, and we knew it was Sowzy.

"The pig is out," I explained to Dr. Loft.

I went outside, and there was Sowzy, pinkly luminous in the moonlight, peering wistfully at me. In docile fashion she traipsed after me back to the piggery and I shut her inside, with reproaches, and fastened up the door.

It wasn't more than forty minutes later that we heard Sowzy on the prowl again. An intuitive flash illuminated me and I said, "I'll tell you what, I think Sowzy must be in heat."

Back to the piggery I took her once more and propped a makeshift brace against the door she had been forcing—a feat she had never attempted before. And again, after a while, we were interrupted by the sounds of her plaintive quest. We reconciled ourselves to the fact that the pig was out for the night, and our evening with the visiting clergyman continued to be punctuated by the explorations and laments of a love-lorn sow.

Next morning, aided by Dr. Loft, who had been a Mid-western farm boy in his time, I reinforced the piggery doors so there could be no recurrence of her roaming. I've wondered, since, if Dr. Loft has ever been able to look at his finished book without remembering the amorous plaint, under the moon, of the Fullers' white sow.

As quickly as possible we sent for a pickup truck with a crate designed for such purposes and dispatched Sowzy to a farm near Middlebury to be bred. She was to board there for several weeks while nature took its course. By this time Sowzy had passed into a manic phase, and the job of cajoling her three hundred pounds up a couple of planks and into a crate was something to reckon with. But we saw her on her way to the trysting place and looked forward hopefully to the fruits of the coming spring.

Her chauffeur for the occasion was a gentle town character of arrested intelligence, a local "Mr. Dick" reminiscent of *David Copperfield*. He had a dim and slightly muddled mind, a stumbling speech, an amiable smile. He could drive well—better than many who were brighter—and was a respected and useful citizen of the town.

In January, only a short time after Sowzy had come back

from her boarding and breeding, we had a visit from our old friend Bertha Krantz. Bert had first been my secretary, then my assistant, in the office days. It was one day during the course of that visit while either Ann or I was slopping the pig, as they say thereabout, that we discovered Sowzy was under the weather. She had got out a few days before, in the snow, to watch Graham skiing, and was a comic image of pink on white until we chased her in again. That may or may not have contributed to the trouble.

Her appetite was poor—an especially ominous symptom in a pig—and she seemed stiff, rheumatic, in her hindquarters. This rotund, amiable, but inherently undignified creature had a kind of antic melancholy about her, sitting on her haunches, peering at us dolefully with grunts of mild complaint.

We were alarmed and began to cast about in our minds whether to reproach ourselves for letting her catch cold by failure to keep the piggery sufficiently tight and warm—as with the calves who had come to such a crisis before Christmas. The idea of moving her in to live with them was preposterous. Possibly she had picked up some infection during her sojourn away for breeding. In any event, as so many times for so many creatures, we summoned Dr. Miller, for whom I was beginning to feel we constituted a complete practice.

He came in the early afternoon with his burly helper. Ann, Bert, and I accompanied them into the piggery, peering over the barrier anxiously. Miller observed Sowzy's stiff motions and managed to take her temperature. She was running a fever. He wanted to give her both a hypodermic injection of penicillin and some sulfa pills. Sowzy, meanwhile, was becoming increasingly nervous and agitated.

The doctor made a quick stab at her haunches with the

hypodermic, scoring successfully, though Sowzy uttered a shriek of outrage. Then we came to the rough going. The vet was determined that Sowzy must have the sulfa pills. It was necessary to use the long injector to thrust them down her throat, as I had seen him do before with the cows. The problem was to hold Sowzy down and get her jaws open.

She was not going to have any of it. Dr. Miller, who had a game leg, and the burly helper advanced purposefully upon her. Sowzy began to dash about her pen wildly—it was perhaps some twelve by twelve—and she set up the frightful, hysterical shrieking that few creatures can match, unless it be trumpeting elephants. It had been laughable when we were catching young shoats by their hind legs and heaving them into gunny sacks. But with Sowzy, now, there was a more strident note of stark panic, ear-piercing and emotionally upsetting. We felt that it just was not right.

The girls looked on the maneuvers with a kind of horror, and I, who had been keeping out of the way, now entered the pen to lend some added muscle, but also in hope that my familiar presence might calm Sowzy a bit.

She was over the hill. Her shrieks, with their dismayingly human quality, were among the most distressing sounds that I have ever heard. Every time we closed in on her, three hundred pounds of hysterical pig launched itself at our legs and bowled us over. There was no malice in her—just fear.

By now I wanted to call a halt to the whole thing but was constrained, as we sometimes are with doctors even about beloved people, by the feeling that the experts, the professionals, have taken over and who are we to interfere? Sometimes one must.

Finally we got Sowzy cornered more thoroughly than we had been able to do before. I had a secure grip on her hind legs. Miller's helper had tackled her just behind the forelegs. The doctor was attempting to force a loop of cord into her mouth with which to pry open her jaws. Just what symptom he saw I do not know, but suddenly he called out, "Let her go! Let her go!" The command was so peremptory that we obeyed it instantly.

Sowzy, heaving and gasping hoarsely, swayed for a moment, then abruptly fell over on her side with a heavy thump. There were a couple of reflexive leg kicks—and she was stone-cold dead.

All of us simply stared. Each of us understood what had happened. The dreadful exertions of panic and the corpulence of her kind had combined to destroy her. Sowzy had dropped dead of a heart attack.

I felt like a murderer. I would have done almost anything to reverse the clock a half-hour and put my foot down against this chase and wrestling match with Sowzy, to let her take her chances with the medication we could give her peacefully. Take the lesson we learned painfully: Don't fight a pig. Nobody can win.

Dr. Miller, a conscientious vet, was chagrined and shaken. He kept repeating, "I never saw anything like it! She went just like that!" He had succeeded with those tactics before, but I was convinced that he would never try them again. After a few moments of oppressive postmortem reflections, Dr. Miller and his helper departed. I was left with a hard and sorry job to do.

Ann, Bert, and I were all deeply downcast. Fortunately Meredith was up at the brick house and the boys were in school.

The tenth day of January is not the best time to bury a hog in Vermont. Sowzy was extraordinarily heavy. I had been too flustered to think of having Miller's helper aid us in getting her out. Each taking a leg, Ann and Bert helped me drag her outside and around the corner of the piggery to the edge of the pasture. We rolled her under the fence there.

Though we had been through bitter weather, the last couple of days had been relatively mild. I broke the two or three inches of hard-frozen ground with a pickax, and although nothing was soft, the undersurface was easier to handle after that.

A sow of three hundred pounds takes a good deal of burying. Ann had the unrelenting chores of the house calling her. Bert, snugly bundled up, gamely stuck it out beside me while I played my long, slow grave-digger scene. By the time the boys got home to hear the sorry news the job was done. It was the end of Sowzy and the finale of our pig-raising enterprises. It seemed an awful combination of waste and bungle—but by then we were finding our world to be full of both.

CHAPTER ELEVEN

Fire and Ice

LET US NOT ROMANTICIZE. Winter in the blockhouse was grim. We went through three of them before we wintered in the brick house. While brick walls and the oil furnace did not modify the outside rigors, indoors they made a world of difference.

A relative of Nathan Hand went to visit him in the blockhouse, in 1799, and wrote a letter back to Rhode Island: "Notwithstanding the severity of ye winters, it is healthy. I have been full as well since being here as I was at Newport. Snow comes very often, but not in the manner they do with us. They are not attended with high wind, consequently they drift but very little which make fine slaying & ye whole country is continually slaying backwards & forwards. We have a steady cold, not as changeable as with us. We have not cold sharp easterly winds. Ye people are not apt to get colds. No fogs, the weather is very uniform. They will set out upon a journey of 150 miles when it snows. The pleurisy is not known here."

We had been encouraged by the idealistic view of block-house winters thus conjured up. It was true that we did not know the pleurisy, but either the letter writer was a poor ob-server of the winds or there had been a drastic shift of weather patterns in something over a century. The wind was our despair.

The blockhouse had been built to resist Indians, animals, and any other enemies that might be around. It still would have been dandy for that, but those dangers were not our problem any more. If ever the structure had resisted the teeth-chattering, bone-shaking winds that roared continually off the western mountains and across the frozen lake to hit us with full momentum, it had lost that capacity now.

Both of us, but Ann especially, have an antipathy to wind, and can stand almost anything but continual blowing. It was so constant on the farm and so bitter in the winter that when we spoke of a day as windy, we meant it was at high gale force and you could scarcely stand against it, even if it had been warm. The whispers and sighs within were like a haunted house, the setting for a Gothic horror tale. Recurrent diary pages begin with the laconic "Wild wind all night." There was an evening when I was milking and the relentless, veer-ing, buffeting gusts were causing the old barn to groan, creak, and sway so badly that I was downright frightened, for a good many tons of baled hay were above my head.

Against these winds the blockhouse was inadequate in spite of the extraordinary structure whence its name derived. Out-side it looked like a small clapboard salt box. Only the size of the chimney that thrust through the pitched slate roof, dead center, distinguished it externally from thousands of rows of imitations in depressing developments.

Inside, when the walls were stripped for furring and insulating paper to be applied prior to wallboard, the basic structural walls turned out to be unlike anything we have ever seen. They were planks, for lack of another name, cut by Samuel Herrick from the virgin pine of the pre-Revolutionary wilderness. These were five inches thick, eighteen inches wide, and some ran the length of the house. Of course they were laid up edgewise, from sills to eaves. Probably the house had stood unclapboarded for years. The original window and door piercings must have been minimal; one door only, I am sure. In modern times a second door had been cut, and many windows. Up in the wasted corners of the eaves were many of the vast blocks that had been sawed from that primeval planking to make new window openings. We showed these giant blocks proudly as curiosities.

During the stripped-down period of the inside refinishing, the shell was an impressive sight, but not the only one. The central chimney, formidable enough from the outside, was monstrous. It was brick, with black marble hearths of some later vintage. It had openings in four rooms. The north side, which became our dining room, had a great walk-in fireplace with kettle crane and a deep Dutch oven on its left side. Our bedroom on the east had a good fireplace, as did the living room on the west. The small south room we converted into an L of the living room. There opened into the chimney from it a large meat-smoking chamber that had certainly seasoned many a ham with smoke from the abundant hickory on the farm.

The second story was small, cramped by the sloping roof. But from it we eked the bathroom, two small bedrooms for the children, and a little storage. The vast chimney rose bare in the center, and from the floor level was tiered back sharply, to cut its size at the roof. It always brought a gasp from visitors on first sight. There was a blocked-up fireplace on the west side upstairs, too, and a flue opening which later took the pipe from a Coleman kerosene stove.

All advisers had agreed that installing central heating in this odd and ancient structure would be prohibitively costly. Initially our heat was supposed to be from the Coleman stove upstairs, a coal- or wood-burning kitchen range downstairs, and the fireplaces. Soon we added a modified potbellied coal stove—actually an antique with considerable charm to which we rapidly became coldly impervious—in the living room. It could cast a good deal of heat and sustain it. Still later, in real desperation, instead of attempting to use the dining-room fireplace, we inserted part way into it a large tin chunk stove, the pipe of which ran directly up and into a flue hole.

The house was a labyrinth of multi-elbowed stovepipe. The chunk stove and Coleman stove had fairly short and simple ones. The coal stove in the living room had a long one with three elbows. The longest of all ran from the kitchen range into the same face of the chimney as the chunk stove. It was such a long, twisting pull that the draft never worked well. Ann was goaded into frenzies of cruel frustration trying to cook or bake. Water was slow to boil and the oven could not be coaxed up to three hundred degrees. The stovepipe was re-rigged and repitched repeatedly, and the position of the stove was shifted once to try for improvement. Ann suffered it a long time before we bought an electric range on which she could cope better with a meal.

I made an acquaintance I would be glad to forget with the all-too-frequent grimy chore of taking down the pipes and cleaning them out.

Of all these resources, the Coleman kerosene stove was one of the steadiest functioners, though I suffered from several complexes about it. One was the city man's abiding conviction that it was apt to explode. Filling it was a nuisance and always worried me when the stove was burning. We kept two drums of kerosene, first in the old milk house, and later in the horse barn, and I carried it in for stove filling in a five-gallon can. We could have mounted a drum near the stove upstairs with a feed line, but I was unwilling to do so. There were fire hazards enough, I worried, too—shades of Émile Zola— about a flue block-up or leak and carbon monoxide. Even if trouble of that sort had developed it could well be that enough outside air was always flooding into the house to make my fears unnecessary.

The living-room coal stove was very effective, but dirty. There was endless coal-scuttle hauling, kerosene filling, and wood carrying, much of which inevitably devolved upon Ann during the days when I was either in the barn, up at my study, or sometimes away. The chunk stove, while trouble-some, is a wonderful resource for quick heat. Its thin, tin walls throw heat from the instant of kindling. The problems are its relative fire hazard, the risk of children falling against it, and its appalling voraciousness. The latter means a good deal of ash dumping—an aspect of the coal stove, too, to which is added clinker chopping.

In spite of our intention to supply all our wood needs from the farm, sheer volume of consumption forced us to order mill slabs, from time to time, for the chunk stoves (I installed one in my office, too), and in the worst of the winters I bought some heavy, large seasoned maple chunks with which it was possible to bank even the chunk stove to last the night. We used the bedroom and living-room fireplaces every evening.

I am sure that Samuel Herrick and his successor Nathan Hand, with their families, shivered through many a winter. That optimistic relative of Nathan Hand's in 1799, quoted above, observed, "The winters are severe and long, but they have great plenty of wood and keep noble fires." Having few windows and only one door then, and being relatively new, the house was no doubt a little tighter. We also kept noble fires, but with the best of our efforts, insulation, and all of our heat, we were cold. One walked always through currents and layers of varying temperature in the rooms. Drafts never were wholly suppressed against that fingering, clawing wind.

Our interior water pipes froze periodically (never the ones in the ground). By a mysterious irony of general science the hot-water line always freezes first. On the second floor the pipes ran in the open a foot or so inside the eave line. After several times of having to thaw them at some joint with a blow torch we wrapped them in yards and yards of an electric thermal tape, which helped a little, but we were always subject to a sudden freeze up at the height of the wind, or one of the night drops to a one-time extreme of twenty-six below. Ten to fifteen below was common and on a few, happily rare, bad stretches there would be night-day-and-night sequences never struggling above zero.

I have observed a certain meteorological competitiveness deep-grained in the human race. In all extremes of weather, as neighbors meet in general stores, post offices, or filling stations, there is an avid contest for records. "It was five below here this morning!" "That so? It was fifteen below over to our place." The same thing goes on in the summer on the upper range of the thermometer.

Every winter in the blockhouse, on the worst of the wild nights, Ann and I would "fire-sit." It was an absolute necessity. If we banked the fires in the ordinary way under such circumstances, the cold would soon pierce the house. Fires had to be kept at peak, and for good cause based on experience we could not all sleep, especially with our three children upstairs, not only needing to be kept warm, but sleeping in a potential firetrap.

There was a morning at breakfast, in the bitter cold, when one of the children screamed and pointed. Where the chunk-stove pipe entered the flue the wall was burning, in spite of protective collar and insulation. It was the result of hours on end of force firing the stove. We put it out ourselves after minor damage—chiefly to the paint—but we were haunted by the possibility of such an occurrence at night with all asleep.

So it was that on the bad stretches Ann and I would divide the night, alternately sleeping half the night and sitting up, fire tending, the other half.

On January 30 of the first winter, a Sunday with icy roads, Ann had stayed home with Meredith and I was at church with the boys. I sang in the choir of the village church, which was Congregational. In the midst of the service the fire siren sounded. At nearly the same moment my friend and neighbor, an orchardist, Bill Stalker, appeared at the door, beckoning to me urgently from the back of the church. I marched out at once.

Bill said, "You've got a chimney fire. Better come with me, I've got chains on."

I was too frightened of what might be happening at home to be frightened of Bill's fast, slithering drive, chains notwithstanding. As we came along the road by the high pasture, we could see volumes of yellowish smoke pouring from the chimney but no sign of anything worse. The fire engine had beaten us there and the yard was full of men. Ann, Meredith, and Virginia were all standing by. Meredith was crying and I learned later that for some odd reason, like horses in a burning barn, she showed a persistent tendency to run back in the house, if released. A few moments after my arrival Walt Bryant came from the church, driving my car and bringing the boys.

I was given some quick assurances, and went in with some of the men to see what was up. Inside there was a tremendous, vibrating roar, the beginning of which had alerted Ann to what was happening. That cavernous chimney, multiflued, was like a blast furnace. On the second floor the brick was too hot to touch and there was a scorched smell. From invisible chinks in the brickwork, enough smoke was seeping to impart a smoky atmosphere but not to threaten damage.

All the men, many of whom had worked on the house for us, were agreed on basic policy. To use water would destroy the chimney and, in effect, the house. They were watching the roof and all frame connections for fire, and if these did not catch, the best thing was to let the chimney burn itself out, which would clean it as nothing else could.

When we had opened it up and rigged stoves, the flues were functionally clear and had been brushed out some. But this vast honeycombed ancient chimney evidently was full of shelves and pockets with soot accumulations, with probably inches of hard deposit built up along the sides of flues that still had ample open throats. Our many sustained fires had simply built up a heat point at which the whole thing got going.

It burned for hours and slowly died out. A couple of men stood by until it seemed to be slacking. We observed it closely after that. It was twenty-four hours before we could lay a hand on the bricks, which stayed hot, slowly diminishing to warm, for days afterward.

Ann had been through an ordeal. When she began to realize what was happening she snatched up the frightened, resisting Meredith and started up the snowy hill for the brick house, for we had no phone in the blockhouse. (Because of this day's events we installed one.) But the phone at the brick house failed to work—it was a primitive, hand-cranked wall box. Ann got out Virginia's car, with difficulty, and drove the mile or so up to the Stalkers to phone the fire department from there. Then she came back and Bill made his dash to the village to get me.

Both physically and emotionally it had been traumatic for Ann. Retrospectively we have always wondered if that Sunday contributed in some way to a miscarriage which she suffered less than two months later. It was not a provable matter.

In my remodeled granary office up the hill I had heating problems, too. Between its structural beams, interior wallboard had been applied, giving a pleasing timbered effect. Yet on the whole, from its very nature and the fact that the building stood on legs and the floor was not insulated, it was less tight than the blockhouse. Sometimes I worked in conditions in which I could see my breath and had fingers too stiff to type or hold a pencil well.

Originally I had thought to heat the office by a coal stove, almost a twin of our living-room one, on the first floor. The pipe rose straight up through the second floor, where my desk was, and out the roof. The rising pipe radiated heat and I expected some to rise through the open stairs. Although the coal stove was valuable in that I could keep some sort of warmth banked there, it was most inadequate. I added a chunk stove on the second floor, its pipe entering the other one by a T joint.

That chunk stove, like the other, ate fuel insatiably while I was trying to write. To eke it out, I did something about which I felt faintly guilty for a long while, simply because of the sound of the matter. I burned books.

In the attic and in several big old bookcases that had come with the house, there were great quantities of old books, many of them in decaying, pulverized, or cracked leather bindings. Others were in dreary old cloth. Some were rat-gnawed, stained, and faded; some, not in bad shape. It was among these books, when farm hunting, that I had seen the symbolic set of *Fuller's Works,* which I preserved with some others, such as Carpenter's account of his stay in the White House while painting Lincoln and his cabinet, and a small collection of other worth-while items, including Fuller & Wayland, *On Domestic Slavery.*

If you think me barbaric for my book burning, I can only say as a passionate booklover that I felt justified. I had combed through those volumes many times with a knowledgeable bookman's eye. The rest were the main bulk of attic junk which, after an occasional pearl has been culled, as I culled a few, cannot be palmed off anywhere. Every second-hand dealer knows that. They are the sort of things which sometimes are dumped as contributions on the doorsteps of despairing librarians who know that they have only inherited the task of having them hauled away and junked. They can't be sold for a penny apiece at church rummage sales.

That was the kind of books I burned. There were a lot of them. *Whelpley's Compendium* was a typical example. As a bookman I felt an analogy to the proper respectful disposal of

worn-out flags, Bibles, and paper money—all objects of veneration in the American way. They are not to be degraded
upon trash heaps and dumps, but should be cleanly, decently,
honorably cremated. A book is slow-burning, even when dry
with age. Once my chunk stove was going I would feed in a
few volumes from time to time. For a man writing new books
by their heat it was chastening to poke up the fire and see
their pages flutter and glow, the ink of the print now fiery on
the ashen paper. It was like the symbolic burnings of flax in
Papal coronation processions, accompanied by the admoni-
tory words: "*Sancte pater, sic transit gloria mundi.*"

Of all the collection only one title, a compact book in excellent shape with a gold-lettered leather spine, escaped me. I
don't think it went into the fire, but however it happened it
got away somehow and I cannot forget it. It was one of a
numerous, once-popular genre, the posthumous oddments of
sermons and other pious literary fragments of deceased di-
vines. This one was called *Smellie's Remains.* Would that I
had it back!

Graham and I had our winter struggles in the barn. The
crux of them was two-fold—manure and water.

Barn routine is an absolute tyranny. It cannot be avoided,
except rarely by foisting it off on someone, but there it is,
twice a day, demanding to be done. One could always set fire
to the barn and leave.

The winter routine with our own milking stock (which
reached a maximum of four) and the unbred heifers that we
always wintered for Ollie Farnham or somebody, went thus:
up at five-thirty in the bitter blackness; over to the barn,
sometimes in deep snow or driving sleet; then the milking.

All the cattle had developed heavy coats. In the winter

conditions they got very dirty. Before milking there was vigorous bag washing to be done and the hot water carried over in pails from the house for that purpose was soon cold. Hands would get icy and cracked in this job—and the cracks would sting. To get the fingers flexing to milk was hard going. The very process was helpful but still painful. We milked, huddling into the flank to avoid slaps in the face from a heavily caked tail.

The first winter, Susan and the calves got a case of barn itch—a kind of winter mange. We had to treat this added complication by rubbing into their coats a heavy, greasy, yellowish, stinking ointment, which we had to make ourselves from powdered sulphur and lard—as unlovely a mix as you will find, with no future in the cosmetic field.

After milking we turned out all the critters, with the exception of penned calves, into the barnyard to mill around for exercise and to drink. Before turning them out, however, we had one of the naturally nastiest of all jobs to do. There had never been water in our barn. Even if slate ledge had not prevented our running the pipes there without prohibitive cost, at no time did we ever have a sufficiently tight barn with an adequate population of stock to keep it warm enough for running water.

All we had was our six-foot-diameter, three-foot-deep galvanized-iron tub, which sat flat on the ground just inside the fence. A deep-layed pipe from the pond ran through our cellar and over to the tub, beside which it rose straight into the air and curved over the side. It was cunningly pitched, in the laying, to drain back into our cellar. In winter we never shut it off at the tub. Each morning we had to trot back, turn it on in the cellar, let it run as long as needed, then go back to the cellar, turn it off, and open the little drain-off valve so that there would be no water standing in that outside pipe to freeze.

It was a constant, agonizing fight to keep the tub from freezing solid. In the bitter weather Graham and I would attack it with two weapons: my eight-pound sledge hammer, which I still have and with which I still split wood, and a massive crowbar, which I also still have, taller than I am. We would have to shatter the coat of ice, then with a many-tined manure fork fish out the chunks or flat cakes and throw them as far off to the side as we could. They built into an ice hill as winter wore on.

But there were many mornings when the heaviest, repeated sledge-hammer blows simply bounced back with a nasty splat and thud, spraying stinging pellets of mashed ice into our faces. In a long operation this splatter would freeze on our clothes like chain mail. Then we would climb right up on top of the tub and with the crowbar chip and chip and chip. Often it was necessary to sink several crowbar holes in a pattern and then smash out the center piece with a hammer blow. Occasionally we employed a pickax as well, which cruelly peppered the face with ice. Once we had cleared as much as we could, we ran in water to a sufficient level and turned out the critters. They drank a great deal but over a period of time, during which sometimes the surface would begin to glaze over in rapid order.

We had to leave the tub full to the brim, or, by getting shallow, it would freeze solid. But our great problem was side-freezing. The ice would thicken from the sides inward and all the way to the bottom. We were driven toward an ever-contracting center which after a while would get out of reach of the cattle. This was almost impossible to chip away, though we always used crowbar and pickax to get rid of whatever we could.

On a few occasions the awful cold would catch us with a pipe freeze beside the tub, for all our best precautions. Then we would have to pile up wood, pour on kerosene, and set a fire going to thaw it out. This stratagem we had to employ on a more massive scale against the sides of the tub, to break the fearful bonding of the ice against them and give us a chance to crack and chip the ring so we could get out some sizable chunks. We looked like arctic cannibals around a vast cauldron when at this operation. Because of the labor and appalling time consumption of this task we seized every slight natural thaw to rid that tub of ice whenever we had a break.

But we still haven't got to the end of the morning routine. Once the cattle were all milling around the barnyard for their water, we had to get the manure out the west side of the barn where the piles accumulated.

The gutters of the barn were warped, lumpy, or sprung in places, which never made it easy to get a long running thrust down the gutter with the manure shovel. Also, because of our light population and minimal animal heat, the manure tended to freeze in patches and that was a nasty problem in chipping, for to let it go cumulatively would be disastrous.

Graham, in those winters at ten, eleven, and twelve years, worked valiantly but with natural limits. He had to break off, wherever we were, in time for a quick breakfast and cleanup, and to catch the school bus. Chores were waiting for him again when he got home. I was a dogged but not highly efficient worker. These chores were a long time getting done, longer than would be the case with a skilled farmer, proper equipment, and perhaps a hired man.

In the final winter, when we were milking four, by machine, and I was selling a can of milk a day at the creamery, the chores were that much more protracted, involving the hot-water scrub-up of the machines in the milk house, then the heaving of the big milk can into the trunk of my car, which often wouldn't start, and delivery to the milk plant three miles away.

It would easily be ten or ten-thirty when I staggered in, theoretically due to proceed to my office and really earn my living, but sometimes in fact to fall face-down over the bed and go to sleep. Then, of course, the essential routine, only slightly less than that of the morning, would begin again at four or four-thirty in the afternoon.

There is a classic tale about a farmer and a city man comparing the relative rigors of their working days. "I work from nine to five," the city man said. "I work from nine-thirty to four," the farmer said. "Why," said the city man, "I've driven past your farm often and seen the lights on in the barn at six in the morning and at seven in the evening." "Oh, well," the farmer said, "you gotta do the chores."

This combination of duties and the chronic harassments with the car is reflected typically in excerpts from a February 21 diary entry:

Chores. Tired. To study to work all morning. Battery dead so Ann towed me out with Virginia's car but could not start and got mired on bend. After lunch Farr's truck came and towed me out, not starting till near Stalker's. But battery so low starter wouldn't work and had to run engine for hours in hope of charging it enough. More work in study. Cleaned calves and toted hay, boys helping. Chores. To bed early.

In addition to the unvarying demands of the house and of feeding us, Ann was frequently involved in the other chores. She learned to milk, always handled the calves when they were very young, and pitched in with any phase of chores, simply to help or to release me for some other essential task, or because I was ill or away.

Winter in Vermont, then, was not a joy to us, for the reasons spelled out. But nothing is a total pattern, and there were moments of fun and some experiences of cold beauty that lifted the weary spirit.

The very first Christmas on the farm, sleds, skis, and skates were main motifs. The roads and meadows offered slopes for the former. In addition to the relatively tame but comfortably handy skating on our pond, there were always a few times a winter when the lake had a good snow-free surface. That made adventuresome skating with miles of range. Once the boys and I skated all the way down opposite the Fort where the Revolutionary wartime bridge of boats had linked the Fort and Mount Defiance on the west side, with Mount Independence on the east. Sometimes the wind was so rough that we would find ourselves with all the effects of sail skating *sans* sail, and an iceboat would have been high sport. But among the pitfalls of lake skating was the danger of letting oneself reach the extreme tolerance of coldness while still on the ice, and then be faced with the long, wind-swept trek back up to the house.

For work or play, indeed even for the house, we all wore good old-fashioned long underwear, stopping short of sewing ourselves into it for the season. At an army surplus store in New York, before we moved, I had gone berserk and bought winter equipment that would have been suitable on Scott's last expedition. This included white canvas parkas that tied at neck, sleeves, and waist, and heavy army green woolen gloves that ran well up the arm. Funniest but still useful, itchiness notwithstanding, was a head-fitting knitted pull-over, extending down to neck and shoulders, with merely an oval cutout for the face. It gave a pronounced medieval impression.

Dressed in this sort of rig, I went down to the lake one day after chores, with Ann's encouragement. We could see some men fishing out on the ice, and this was an operation I had not yet viewed. It turned out to be the local builder of my rowboat and a father and son from Rutland.

In a most friendly fashion they showed me the technique of cutting a hole with an ice-chisel and setting up a tipup. This is a little wooden rig, straddling the hole, to which the line is fastened. When there is a bite, or even much of an inquiring nibble, a flag is tipped up to alert the fisherman. They set me up with a line, minnows, and tipups, and I fished with them all day but caught nothing. Since no skills were involved once the line was set, it was fortune and not virtue that netted the others several two- to three-pound walleyes.

Once the ice had a permanent look to it, the shanties appeared for the serious fishing. These resembled portable privies, on runners, and were of varying sizes and degrees of luxury. They gave shelter from the unceasing wind, and because they generally had a bit of floor, relieved the feet from the constant contact with the ice, which managed to make itself felt gradually through the heaviest boots and socks. The shanty would be centered over a good-sized hole in the ice—a hole in the shanty floor corresponding to it. From the shelter, too, one could keep an eye on a network of outside tipups.

When Mr. Gregoire got his shanty down there I spent some time with him, and he gave me several fine walleyes from his own superflux one day when, as Tommy would have put it, they were bitin' pretty rank. Tommy was too lazy to have a shanty.

The permanent appearance of the ice was always a speculation. A lucky or alert fisherman would get on and off unscathed, sometimes several times in a season. Whenever there was a quick thaw and a rain—especially late in the season, those who could would come running to drag off the shanties —which sometimes froze in and wouldn't budge. Each winter several were lost, and one or two wrecked shanties along my shoreline, perhaps from miles up lake, were par each spring after the final breakup.

When the lake was firmly set, cars and even trucks were driven blithely over it; many shanties were taken out that way. A road was always established over the ice to Ticonderoga in the same place that the ferry plied. We made the drive a couple of times but it always made me nervous, even though I had heard of cars driving across the Gulf of Finland. It was possible to lose a car through the ice.

The indoor pleasures of the winter, to compensate partially for the harassments, were all of the wholesome, folksy, John Greenleaf Whittier genre. Popcorn and chestnuts and cider, or any hot drink on a cold night had their comforts. When you heard the wind roaring, warmth was a positive goodness even if—rather, especially if—hard bought. Yet Ann came, at last, to share Scott's stark words, written down at the South Pole: "My God, this is an awful place!"

But the visible winter beauties are the final aspect of the picture. It was a Grandma Moses world at times, and then also something more starkly and austerely lovely. In the cove and woods were the skeletal ghosts and wraiths of plants. And in the winter the mountains and hills showed not just their surface but their architecture.

A February 6 diary entry begins:

Up at 6:00 to milk. 14 below. Most beautiful winter morning we have ever seen. Every tree and every filament heavy with dazzling white frost. Air dry and snapping. Sights magnificent.

The night landscapes, too, were superb. The ghostly Adirondack ranges in the full moon seemed like a floating illusion in the sub-zero clarity of the air. The winter nights sometimes orchestrated themselves, as it were, to a measure that went beyond beauty to the awesome.

I'm sorry for someone who has never wintered close to a large body of water that freezes deep. The weird music of the ice is eerily fascinating. Lake Champlain was a mighty instrument. When the ice sheet had formed so thick that cars could be driven across it, it had a gamut of stress noises of remarkable variety. These proceed primarily from the expansion or contraction of the ice between the changes of air temperature above it and, no doubt, water movements or temperature variations below it.

Its cracking noises would range from sharp pistol-shot effects to reverberant cannon booms. There would be splinter noises that vibrated at the end like a slightly sprung tuning fork. It would be like the mysterious distant noise that casts a spell of melancholy portent over the characters of *The Cherry Orchard* in the last act, with a suggestion of some vast harp-string snapping. Other times it would groan like an animal. It would sing with sustained minor-key cadences that sounded to me, then, like a musical saw, but by more modern reference like some of the effects in electronic music. If you were on the lake when this was going on, it was not only heard but felt as the ice quivered or jarred with shock.

One of the best times for this lake recital, which could often be anticipated, was in the early dark of a still night when, from the moment of sunset, the temperature began a plunge into the sub-zeros. The lake then would quicken and run through its full repertoire. There were several nights in those winters, when these sound effects were accompanied by exceptional auroral displays, rippling across the zenith, forming and re-forming as curtains or shafts, and sometimes seeming to flow outward in circular concentric waves from a center directly overhead. The aurora was mostly white but was occasionally a pale-green wash, purple, amber, or faintly red. Stars were visible through the veils of light. Sometimes I saw these displays still flickering when I rose before dawn for chores. Once, in utter prodigality, all these effects were combined with an eclipse of the moon.

All of us would stand outside, briefly impervious to the dry bite of the cold, and gaze at the celestial spectacle accompanied by the sepulchral music of the lake. I've known no other natural phenomena to top it. The scalp would prickle with awe—that high fear of immense and noble mystery—at this direct communication from the universe.

CHAPTER TWELVE

My Life with
the Inseminator

INSEMINATOR was the chastely clinical, altogether fitting and proper name for him—identifying at a stroke both the person and his function. Privately I always thought of him formally as "Mr. Inseminator," partly from awe, partly because the title fell upon my inward ear with the pleasing, nostalgic cadence of that vanished high functionary of old-time minstrel shows: Mr. Interlocutor.

He was the embodiment of a new era in animal husbandry, of a technology responsible for a general improvement of dairy stock, a corrective to excessive inbreeding, and a banisher of that always dangerous because often underestimated creature, the farmyard bull. That animal's frequent surliness was often aggravated by his being tethered thoughtlessly by nose ring and chain in the sun. In folklore he was the bane of the unwary who ventured to cross broad pastures believed to harbor nothing but peaceably grazing cows.

The barnyard scene was changing, as I had learned from farm pamphlets and expert advice long before the first time it became necessary to assuage the renewed mating urges of Susan, who had been with calf when we acquired her.

A cow comes into heat every twenty-one days but there are not always clear signs thereof, as nature seems to lie dormant sometimes. Susan had shown no symptom of such a state for months after Daisy was born. But when she began to respond, her big-eyed, long-lashed mask of Victorian demureness vanished. If bulls would not come to her she would hunt for bulls. She took off over the barbed-wire fence one time, scratching her bag nastily, and turned up, bawling, nearly two miles away outside our neighbors, the Marceaus', barn.

The strident bawl—*"booooooooo-awwwwwwwwww!"*—with which Susan made hideous the air astonished us, like so many other firsts on the farm, when at last she took notice of being in heat. She became a bovine bacchante. The cry rose out of the deepest chambers of her being: direct, urgent, elemental. There was no beast at hand to respond to this siren song. Instead, I hurried to the phone to call the regional Artificial Breeders Association. That was when Mr. Inseminator came into Susan's life and mine.

He was a young man, laconic and brusque, with a jumpiness that was not vulgar nerves but an extreme intolerance of any kind of time wasting or delay—especially that which arose from bumbling questions of the sort that I was apt to stand by and ask. I came to learn that this was his occupational hazard. He had a lot of territory to cover, to attempt to reach all calls within the relatively brief period of actual fertility from the time he was notified of the symptoms, and it became clear later that he endured much in the way of delaying phone calls or from inexact information left for him.

Whenever you spoke to him, even quite intelligently and legitimately, he seemed straining to get on. He would listen quiveringly, with lid-lowered eyes, cloaking an infinite exasperation behind an unconvincing masquerade of infinite patience. He did not suffer fools gladly, and it was clear that fools populated his world.

That first day I hovered by, fascinated. Pursuant to prior briefing I had confined Susan in the stanchion and the barn was vibrant with her calls. Also, I had provided a pail of water for ablutions in the mystic rites. Fetching this or that for him, at crisp commands, to justify my unwanted presence, I was an acolyte to the priest of a fertility cult.

We wanted Susan bred this time to a Jersey bull, in an effort to work back along her involved genetic detours toward the cow of our dreams. Since the least said about her lineage the better, there was no need to have pedigree papers filled out—a necessary part of many of his calls, including later ones to us for our purebred heifers.

The Inseminator carried a case containing bottles of semen from several sires of various breeds. Rubber-aproned and rubbed-gloved, he drew up an adequate portion of the vital fluid into a long plunger and propelled it deep into the proper passage. Susan was marvelously docile, though it was clear that one of the Inseminator's occupational hazards, against which he was booted and aproned, was a cow's simple-hearted penchant for defecating or voiding urine at any crucial moment, from milking to medical ministrations. I had come to regard this response almost as a bovine vote of confidence, a testimonial that the situation was normal. Show me a cow that doesn't do at least one or the other almost every time you're standing by—especially with city visitors—and I'll show you a dead cow.

Now when the Inseminator had completed his quick but

skillful act Susan remarkably lapsed at once from her clamor into a munching serenity. As the technician began a brisk washing-up of his instruments and himself I was thrown into meditation.

What had Susan been hollering for? Lewd fellows of the baser sort would have asserted that she wanted the amorous joys tacitly promised to cows by the old-time Bull Durham tobacco billboards. But clearly the unerotic ministrations of the Inseminator had satisfied her. Touchingly, impressively, something in the bovine female essence of Susan knew that it had what it wanted and turned off the alarm. I was more awed by this than by any other aspect of the experience.

The Inseminator zoomed off to carry his precious gift to other waiting cows uttering their plaints throughout the county. I remained beside Susan, touched with a faint melancholy. Whether Susan felt it or not, *I* felt she was missing something. The heat of nature had yielded to the technician's cool touch. I felt intimations of the brave new world and the test-tube baby. I knew that I wanted no AMA equivalent of Mr. Inseminator someday doing my office for me under clinically controlled conditions.

Also I felt the loss of one of the great bawdy folk media of sex education, though an abundance of other barnyard and assorted domesticated critters remained to fill the gap. But all these ruminations stamped me for the amateur and outsider that I was; certainly they were not preying on the mind of a single working farmer.

The fact was that humble Susan, like countless better cows of capable farmers of scanty means, was bred to a bull of qualities beyond the wildest measure of any bull that the ordinary farmer could hope to own. A few dollars had bought the seed of a bull worth many thousands.

We had seen immensely valuable bulls at Ira Payne's farm.

He led us to the stall of his prize one, in a wing of his vast barns. Smelling strangers, the bull set up a menacing, bellowing roar that seemed to my myth-steeped mind to echo out of the Cretan labyrinth. It was my first direct sense of the power pent up in these beasts, revealed to me later in all its dangerous dynamics in the bull rings of Mexico and Spain. Yet even the commonplace barnyard bull has killed or maimed many a farmer. There was a fatal goring in the neighborhood while we were in Vermont. Such things were unnecessary hazards and nuisances now, though a good many farmers still kept a bull.

The promise in the advanced technology contributed to our drift into excessive involvement. We had meant to have one single cow to produce milk for the family. When Susan's first calf was born we couldn't resist keeping her, though Daisy was a clod on both sides of her lineage. Susan's second calf, Juniper, the fruit of selective artificial breeding, was a creature of qualities markedly superior to her half-sister.

Also, however modestly, we had been touched by the pure-bred fever. We wanted only the best breeding for Handy and Taffy, whom we had nurtured so heroically. In due course we called in the Inseminator to cater to them, with all the solemn formalities of identifying and recording the breeding lines on the registry papers, which had to be tacked up over the stanchion.

The first of these summonses was one of the many times I riled the Inseminator acutely. All the semen used in artificial breeding was of good stock but there was an especially select reserve for the more aristocratic purebreds which one obtained by asking for a "proven sire." Such a one was a bull whose good works were recorded unto the third and fourth generations in registered births and certified milk yields among his scatter-sown offspring.

Mr. Inseminator arrived for the first service to virginal Taffy, stood among his pails of water, kit open, rubber gloves on, when I asked innocently, "Is this a proven sire?"

Irascibility erupted at once. All I had asked for in my phone call was a Jersey bull. He didn't have a proven sire in the kit. He stripped off the rubber gloves so savagely that I thought he was about to slap me across the face with them and demand formal satisfaction.

"It's all right," I said. "It's not that important."

It was to him. Once I had uttered the words "proven sire," I had to be taught my lesson, had to learn the sacred rituals by which one obtained a proven sire, had to learn the consequences of inexplicit telephone requests—a subject on which he was hypersensitive, as you will see further.

He packed up his semen in his little kit bag—but did not smile, smile, smile. Off he stomped, in spite of my bewildered protests and pleas, and Taffy remained maiden until her next heat.

With Taffy the breeding was successful; but alas, another discovery about highbreeding awaited us. We found that Handy was sterile. Attempt after attempt with her failed. We called the vet into consultation, and he and the Inseminator talked darkly of such technical terms as corpus luteum—the long and the short of it was that handsome, purebred, plump Handy went at last to Ollie Farnham, as high-quality beef for his own table, while humble Susan plodded on, producing both milk and more creatures to be milked. It was also our luck, signifying nothing, that Susan produced heifer calves consistently, while our first eagerly awaited issue from pure-bred Taffy turned out to be a bull. He went early, for veal.

The choleric, prickly Inseminator came and went often over our few years on the farm. I found him always efficient and also unfailingly amusing, quite without his own intention or knowledge. Then, in our last year on the farm, most unexpectedly he sent me a character sketch of himself. That wasn't what it was called or what it was meant to be. It was a mimeographed bulletin, an official communiqué to all participating members of the Artificial Breeders Association of the entire county. It dealt with mundane, practical matters. But the Inseminator's unique voice was heard at once in the all-cap heading that preceded even the formal salutation of "Dear Member":

PLEASE READ CAREFULLY, BECAUSE SOME OPERATING
PROCEDURE MAY DIFFER FROM WHAT YOU ARE
NOW DOING ! ! !

The bulletin was long—five full single-spaced pages. I put it in my archives at once and now offer chosen highlights.

I will attempt to make this a letter to end all letters . . .

First of all, let's start from the beginning: (As of now forget everything you have ever heard, read or thought about the rules and workings of this association.) O.K., now let's meet your Inseminator, who, incidentally is hired to be the Manager of the Unit he has charge of. So, he is not only a skilled technician to breed your cows, but in addition is the manager, bookkeeper and salesman for the association . . .

To get personal for a moment, I would like to clear up a couple of points about myself that seem to have been causing quite a lot of confusion:

I am *not* married.

That is *not* my wife that answers the phone.

I do *not* eat at my home.

I do *not* eat dinner from 12 noon to 1 P.M.

I have *no* regular meals, *no* regular hours, no regular time to quit work, in fact I ain't got nothin' regular.

I tell you these things in order that you may get a clearer picture of the rules and why they must be followed. Some people have thought that they could call at noon, because then I would be at home eating dinner. 'Taint so. My dinner (Midday meal) hour, which lasts 15 minutes by the way, runs anywhere from 10:30 in the morning to 3:30 in the afternoon. I am *always* out working at some farm at 12 noon. I spend from $1700 to $2000 a year on car expenses alone and one year it went up to over $2500 a year, so you can see I can't very well afford to drive extra miles and spend extra money to pick up late telephone calls . . .

Let's take up the mental aspect of the Inseminator concerning late telephone calls. To illustrate, let's take this example:

Suppose you worked for a man, say in haying time and he told you to go out and bring in ten loads of hay, and that when that was done you could start evening chores. O.K., you go get the hay and you are tired and you put the wagon away and put the tractor away and then the man comes out and says: "While I was over in Town this afternoon I happened to think I needed 12 loads of hay instead of 10, go get them, will you?" Well, you don't like it, but you go out and get 2 more loads.

Now suppose the same thing happens the next day and the next, *and the next*. Suppose that goes on for two months. What is your mental attitude going to be? What are you going to tell that man? I bet you couldn't print it in a newspaper.

By this time probably you are cussing me and saying, "Hell Man, I've got my problems too," (but at least you are reading this letter aren't you?)

Finally, after a long discussion of assessments, fees, and basic information about the service, the memorandum closes with instructions about phone calls. Again, merely excerpts:

> If the hired man calls, have him give *only* the name of the member, not his name too. This will avoid much confusion.
>
> Do not start off your message with: "Can you come out to our place today?" Some people call and say:
> "Hey ———, I need you at my place this afternoon," and then hang up. Unless I know the man's name I don't know where to go.
>
> Do not say "Come this morning," or "Come this afternoon." If you tell me when you noticed the cow I'll come when I'm supposed to.

Following his signature is the final line:

> This letter is approved by your Board of Directors.

It is a masterpiece in the fine, clear note of legitimate irascibility. To this day I honor the Inseminator for it. He was capable, candid, and, as befit his calling, spunky.

CHAPTER THIRTEEN

Hay Foot—Straw Foot

THE SECOND SUMMER we took a direct hand in the haying—that is, we did not sell off the hay rights altogether but cut and baled it on shares, keeping half the crop in our own barn. There was all we needed for our own herd and barn boarders, plus many tons which we could hold to sell on the hay market in the course of the winter. The farm produced abundant hay and we saw to it that the quality was kept up, by reseeding our best meadows, fertilizing, and liming.

This hay husbandry required manure also. It is a vital product, strictly home-produced on dairy farms. Knowing we didn't have enough creatures to yield much manure, we inquired naïvely where some might be bought. We never found a farmer willing to part with so much as a single load. I think farmers would sell their families before they would sell manure. Chemical fertilizers, bone fertilizers you could buy—manure, no.

As an old Mark Twain buff I was reminded of his "Black

Forest Romance," in A *Tramp Abroad*. An impoverished suitor for a farmer's daughter is barred because he lacks manure. "What is a man without manure?" the farmer demands. After a long time the suitor accumulates a heap and appears triumphantly to press his courtship, saying, "Come and view the pile!"

Thus our boarding of heifers was important not only for the animal heat they brought to the barn but because the manure they produced was essential to us, being scanty enough as it was. We shoveled this brown gold out the west side of the barn, morning and night, along with the urine-saturated bedding, rich in nitrogen. It all mounted in a steaming pile. It could not be left too long lest all its richness leach into the soil beneath the pile instead of being distributed on the meadows where it was needed.

The best bedding was the yellow straw baled after our co-operative oat plantings were harvested and threshed. They yielded us many sacks of oats for the graining of our cattle, chiefly the milking stock. These bulging grain sacks were stacked like barricades in the old wing of the barn, where they were the food stock of rats and mice and the happy hunting ground of the cats. But there was not enough straw to last a winter, and hay cannot be wasted as bedding unless one has a stock of rain-spoiled hay good for little else. We found it was necessary to order one or two truckloads of wood shavings and chips from the local lumber mills as bedding. We dumped these in the base of our old silo, for which we had no other use, and the shoveling-out of shavings and their distribution by wheelbarrow for fresh daily bedding were part of our winter chores. That, too, of course, built up the manure pile, for it was perfectly good organic matter soaked in the rich chemicals of cows.

The position of any large accumulating manure pile was an important matter because of the potential fire hazard. Big, efficient, modern barns have overhead bucket systems that convey the manure out to piles well away from the building. We had to chuck it as clear of the structure as we could by hand, then we would lay a heavy plank from the sill to the top of the heap and trundle along this runway precariously with the wheelbarrow, to dump it on the farther side. A manure pile generates heat like an atomic pile—though I'll admit the scale is different, and solely for peaceful purposes. But a manure pile allowed to reach critical mass can burn down a barn, just as green hay in the loft can.

As often as we could arrange it, one or another of our co-operating farmers would come down with his manure spreader. I would stand at the pile with my fork and work at the loading of the machine between its tours of the meadows. This went on through winter and early spring.

I remember a balmy spring day when Dan was spreading manure for me. A young French-Canadian farm hand of his was helping me load the spreader. Each time it rolled away this lad, about twenty-two, stood with me and we chatted and ruminated until the spreader came back for the next round.

The ice had gone out recently, and while we stood there the first boat we had seen that season came up the lake—not one of the summer-long procession of barges operating up and down the lake and the canal system from Albany, but a cabin cruiser.

As the handsome white boat went by we remarked how nice it looked upon the blue waters, and the youth said, "I sure would like to go on one of them yatches."

"It would be very pleasant," I agreed.

"I'd like to travel sometime," he went on wistfully. "I'd like to go to Rutland."

Going to Rutland was all of forty miles, with precious little to see when you got there. It astonished me that this could represent the concept of travel—a vision of the greater world —to anybody. There are still pockets of incredible provincialism. The hillbilly phenomenon is not confined to the Great Smoky Mountains. It's not confined to the country, either. Damon Runyon satirized its Broadway equivalents.

The lure of Rutland to the young Frenchman was the Fair, an annual rite of early September. We went to it one year in anticipation of authentic Yankee Americana but we found that the universal honky-tonk had prevailed. True, there were cattle shows, machinery exhibits, quilts, pickles, jellies, and jams, but these were not what had flushed the throngs out of the hills, long-haired and long-jawed.

As we went about comparing light tractors and looking for improved hand churns we found these exhibits adjacent to a midway of shoddy tent shows, where gravel-throated barkers hawked attractions from freaks to strippers. Graham looked just big enough—and big-eyed enough—so that furtive characters said "*Pssstt!*" and beckoned him toward the lurid poster-flanked doors of the girlie-show tents, until I made myself evident as a scowling father. It was not family entertainment.

The Fair was a place where everything was high-priced and nothing was valuable. It was loud. We remembered taking David as a small boy to a firemen's carnival in Nyack. As we approached the lights and the din on a summer evening, he cried out, "Hear the carnival working!" It was working furiously in Rutland. Meredith had her first merry-go-round ride and the boys went on the Ferris wheel, catching from its heights a glimpse of the feature they insisted we must see.

On the race track the Motor Daredevils were performing, popularly known as the Hell-Drivers. We allowed ourselves to be led by the nose, we then paid through it, and entered the grandstand. The Hell-Drivers were public car smashers, a vicarious outlet for every demonic urge that ever seized a man with his hands upon the wheel. They drove old stock cars through brick walls, burning buildings, and into head-on collisions. They drove up and off ramps for crashing broad jumps. The racket was appalling.

The boys reveled in this orgy of wrecking, which fitted the British expression "perfectly smashing!" But Meredith was perplexed. Something deeply rational in her young mind was affronted. When they lined up a procession of overage school buses and attempted leaps over them in cars from a ramp, Meredith abruptly began to cry and said, "Why do they want to wreck the nice school bus?" We couldn't answer the question and had to take her out.

We went away from the Rutland Fair, Ann and I sorrowing at its shoddiness, Meredith bewildered and exhausted, the boys hectically overexcited. I'm sure my young fellow manure-loader would have been thrilled. They had planned it for him.

We learned that the true rural fairs were to be found in the smaller towns. The nicest, most authentic agricultural exposition on a large scale was the Champlain Valley Fair, east of Burlington. We had a special link with it. Our friend Clem Hurd, a painter, was in charge of its art exhibit. David had done some large abstract designs in crayons—he didn't think of them as "abstract," he just did them. Clem liked them and asked him for one, which he proceeded to frame and hang at the Fair.

. . .

Haying was greatly satisfying and many of us bore a hand in it. The operation lasted roughly from mid-June to mid-July. First, Dan would mow and then rake the hay into rows for baling. That was one of the first critical points. The hay must be allowed to dry. It mustn't be baled green. If rained on after being cut, it will lose in quality—according to whether it is sprinkled or drenched; the latter will ruin it— and also the baling will be delayed until it dries. When the baler has done its work the second crisis occurs: the bales must be got into the barn before it rains, for wet bales are always damaged somewhat, and very wet ones are virtually useless, unsalable, and good for nothing but desperation feeding or bedding.

Farmers suffer through their lives from the perverse capacity of skies to dump downpours out of apparent blue as soon as cut hay is drying or bales are waiting in the field. The scriptural admonition "Let not the sun go down upon thy wrath" can be adapted to the farm maxim "Let not the sun go down upon thy bales." Like everyone else who ever harvested hay we had our bad times with thundershowers, but on the whole we were lucky and our hay crop was by far the most substantial annual financial return from the farm. It never made a profit but went farther than anything else toward reducing the deficit.

Our role in the operation began with the baling. A hay baler is a fascinating machine to follow. It straddles raked rows and gathers up the hay. A powerful plunger periodically rams it down a long shaft, each such thrust forming a dense rectangular slab, perhaps four inches thick. These accumulate to a full-sized bale, better than a yard long and weighing somewhere from fifty to sixty pounds. In a neat feat of early automation the baler ties the bale with two strands of twine and shoves it off the rear. A big meadow full of tumbled bales in the wake of the baler is a pleasant sight, but means work.

A large flat-bed truck follows the baler. Generally one skillful loader is aboard it, occasionally two. A couple of men walk alongside, picking up the bales and tossing them onto the truck, where the loader stacks them. Building such a load is no doubt less tricky than building an old-fashioned load of loose hay, but nevertheless it is a skill, like a grown-up game of blocks, to build the load high in such a way that it will not collapse under the inevitable swaying and bumping of the truck through the meadow and up and down hills.

The bales can be picked up by the strings but that is a dubious practice, for sometimes the strings will snap and then there is a scattered bale. There are also bigger balers that pack more densely and bind the bales with wire. These are used where hay is being produced on a large scale, principally for long-distance shipping. The string-tied bales of our kind could be trucked many miles in towering loads, for we sold many such when we hadn't disposed of them all locally.

The easiest way for me to handle the awkward, heavy bales was with hay hooks—the menacing, curved steel prongs jutting from a wooden handle that longshoremen call cargo or freight hooks, and with which they are reputed to fight murderous battles. I would stride along, swing out my arms and clamp into the ends of a bale with my hooks, rear back and heave it up onto the bed of the truck. The hardest struggle was when the load had been built up several tiers and the bales had to be thrown up higher to be grabbed by the truck man.

The muscular reaction to my first day of bale loading was the most spectacular overall stiffening I've ever endured. It wore off fast and led to a fine conditioning. Between that and year-round chores, and wood splitting, and heifer chasing, and fence fixing, the farm made me so healthy that I've yet to get over it after years of sinking back into sedentary ways.

Graham was a good heaver of bales, too. We were both inordinately proud of holding our own, bale for bale, with seasoned loaders. David was too small for it, so he simply road the loads as supercargo, though the youthful giant he became would have been the mightiest loader of us all. Sometimes I drove the truck, but Ann, who is a good driver of any vehicle, also mastered that and drove a great deal with high proficiency so that all male hands could apply themselves to the heaviest work.

Driving the hay truck was no small skill. In the first place it was old, with a worn clutch, worn gears, and worn brakes. It groaned, screamed, and creaked. One cajoled it rather than drove it. The meadow was bumpy and sometimes hilly, so that you were driving uphill, downhill, or sideways along the hill. Go too fast and you would leave the men behind; go too slowly and you would stall. Start or stop with a jerk, or accelerate abruptly, and the load boss, and perhaps the load itself with him, would be pitched off. You had to remember that you were running a platform on which men were moving about and piling up hay bales. You had to allow, too, for the steadily increasing load weight, which always taxed the poor old motor to its limits by the time the cry went up to head for the barn. That trip, sometimes a long distance, was made at a cautious creep.

The glory of haying is the fragrance. It is a sweet thing—an incense to the nostrils—to work in the sun in a field of newly mowed hay. We loved it—the jocular camaraderie, the scent, the sight of green fields rolling down to the gleaming lake.

The flanking mountains grandly framed the scene. The fore-ground was a shifting, sunlit pattern of hay rows, scattered bales, and moving figures, worthy of Brueghel.

The hay was divided by loads—alternately going to our barn and the trip of a mile or so to Dan's. Each time the groaning truck lumbered into the barn with one of our loads, another phase began. Some of us sprang up onto the floor of the cavernous loft to receive the bales as they were tossed up, and to carry them to stack first in the remotest corners. At several places along the walls of the barn, above the cattle stanchions, were trap-door holes. In the winter we scurried up the vertical wall ladders into the loft, through these, and tossed down the number of bales needed for feeding at the moment. It was a part of barn chores that the boys liked best.

We packed the barn to the rafters. Again it was like block building on a giant scale, and pleasant, as the layers mounted, to walk over the springy, rustling firmness of close-stacked, redolent bales. It had been hot enough out in the sun on the meadows. In the loft, under the huge spread of metal roof, it was a do-it-yourself steam room. The sweat streamed and the countless little fragments of hay and seed clung to the body and prickled or itched. Hay dust filled the nostrils and made us sneeze like snuff sniffers. The odor of the hay was so sweetly intense, packed in this heat, that it was almost intoxi-cating.

It was also the hint of a hazard. If the hay had been baled with insufficient drying and curing, it was green. I have opened a few bales that were slightly calcined at the center, showing how close they had come to the spontaneous-combustion point that is the dread of farmers. The hazard is greater with loose hay, for the dense packing of bales makes open combustion much more difficult, though by no means impossible.

The haying season seems to bring barn burnings for two reasons: green hay and lightning. We saw two spectacular barn fires while we were in Vermont, resulting in total loss, which in one instance resulted in the melancholy destruction of a milking herd.

Lightning seems to have an affinity for loaded barns. I'm sure it is simply that barns stand out in conspicuous size and height, unless there is any sort of static factor in the hay, the season of electrical storms happening to coincide with that of haying. We saw spectacular storms, which we enjoyed and watched with profound awe but also with austere pleasure, since none of us happens to panic about lightning. Storms would come off the Adirondacks and over the lake, by day or night, flinging their bolts and striking visibly. We always tried to be out of woods or pastures before the storms broke. It was a lightning region. Samuel Hand reported in a letter on June 27, 1838—right in haying season—that "day before yesterday the mother of an Irish family was killed by lightning, living opposite Pells on the mount [across by Fort Ticonderoga]. Saturday night my old black horse shared the same fate about thirty rods from the house."

Near Middlebury, in our time, two men were carrying a long length of pipe just as a storm was gathering. Lightning struck the pipe and killed both.

Back to our haying: when the lofts had been packed, we filled in the space where the trucks had driven in, from ground level to roof. David loved the haylofts. Like Siamese cats, he loved the highest places available and used to scurry giddily over the rafters to our alarm when there was no hay in the barn for a landing mat.

Dan's best builder of hayloads was a lean, leathery hand
called Alvin. He bossed us with skill, ordering us just when
and where to deliver a bale as the load grew complicated.
They were laid on the truck in intricate patterns so that the
bales would brace one another by their friction. Even so, he
was fallible, or a driver was partly at fault, for once as we had
just started to roll up from the lower meadow with choice
alfalfa bales, the truck swayed heavily. The high-piled load
gave beneath Alvin and with a yell of alarm he was swept
down with it in an avalanche of bales. I heard the shout and
my reflexes worked faster than my mind. We groundlings
scattered wildly, wondering if the whole truck would tip over.
I had been right beside the truck on the downhill side, with a
hand resting on it. I avoided being buried, but as I leaped
away a bouncing bale got me in the back of the knees and
brought me down like a clipped football player.

We frantically dug Alvin out from under the bales, fearful
of what injuries he had suffered. He was lucky that it was
nothing worse than bruises and breathlessness. His scratched
face was purplish, his hair full of hay, but he mustered the
wind for some faint, hoarse, but artistic and devout cursing.

The work of haying and the cussed spirit of the old Vermonter are caught superbly in Robert Frost's poem, "The
Code."

My diary records that on our busiest day we drew over six
hundred bales, which *is* hay. It varied considerably, and there
would sometimes be a lapse of a few days, according to the
weather breaks. Weather signs also determined whether we
should tackle only a small cutting or venture upon a large
one. If the skies looked doubtful we wouldn't risk getting
caught with our hay down.

On the good afternoons when we had finished, caked with sweat and hay dust, we would go through the woods over to the slaty beach and swim. Those were the times when the lake was best.

CHAPTER FOURTEEN

The Life and Death
of Other-Oo

ONE OF THE PRIMARY RATIONALIZATIONS that prompted the
move to the farm was the theory that it would be wonderful
for the children. Of this, like so many other things, one must
say yes and no.

Graham resisted the change—as he did any change—dog-
gedly. David was precisely right for it both in age and temperament. Meredith was too young to feel it deeply—she
grew into the farm. Faith was born there, against a background of some drama, but we left while she was an infant
and of that she has no memories—which cynics have long
called an enviable state.

But Graham, David, and Meredith all have recollections of
their own, and we have ours of them. We had been there
only a little over a month when the woodchuck episode occurred.

The kitchen garden had been begun at once. Virginia discovered that woodchucks were raiding the tender shoots. "Chuckwoods," David had called them when he was smaller, inverting the word just as he did with "munkchips"—the most engaging of small wild creatures, prolific on the farm.

The specific pair of guilty woodchucks were observed to be living under the sheep barn, "handy-by" to the garden, in the Vermont expression. Gregoire's men were busily at work about the place. One of them took to bringing his rifle, to pick off the woodchucks for us, but with all the coming and going the creatures lay low and did their damage at night. So we borrowed two traps and I set them.

The next day I found that I had both woodchucks in a single swoop—a fat and vigorous pair. We set up a great hulloo and Gregoire's man advanced with his rifle to dispatch them. Graham's tender heart was outraged at the prospect of this callous execution. He argued, protested, denounced, and then bodily blocked the way to where the creatures were huddled by the foundations of the barn. He was all set to fling his body down across them and cry, "Shoot if you must!" In this particular crisis David stood by, playing a kind of neutralist Ismene to Graham's passionate Antigone, allowing for the change in sex.

Virginia was disgusted, for while she liked animals in general, she was remorseless on the protection of crops. Gregoire's man combined astonishment with a certain practical contempt; a bleeding heart over a woodchuck was inconceivable to him. Ann and I, sympathetic but seeing the necessities, reasoned and cajoled in vain. It appeared to be a case of shoot all three or spare all three. I was vexed enough not to be altogether sure which option I preferred.

There was only one way out of the impasse: if the creatures weren't to be executed they would have to be transported. I dismissed the rifleman. The woodchucks, each caught by a foot, snarled in self-defense when approached, and they are formidably armed. If left alone, each would ultimately resort to gnawing off its own foot.

I got heavy leather work gloves, though those teeth could bite through them without half trying. Poking around the tool house for some containers, I came up with a battered wire crab trap we had brought from the Hudson River, and an old mailbox.

Graham, his battle won, turned immensely co-operative. With both boys' help, gingerly picking up the creatures by the trap chains while they struggled violently upside down, I lowered each in turn into one of the makeshift receptacles, released the trap and popped on the lid.

We put our wild cargo into the automobile and set off for some practical equivalent of Australia. I drove a matter of three miles to a place near the creamery and pulled off the road at the edge of a woods. The boys and I took our containers several yards into the brush and opened them. The woodchucks were too depressed and humiliated to come out, as if it were an overcast groundhog day, so we dumped them unceremoniously and they bolted.

When we got back to the car I discovered that the rear wheels had sunk into soft ground and would only spin futilely. The boys were trying to push me out when one of the local orchardists drove by, stopped, and gave us a hand. I looked big-eyed and innocent and offered no explanation to gratify his evident curiosity as to what we were doing off the road at this particular time and place.

Home at last, I unburdened myself somewhat luridly on the subject of the whole bloody struggle. Contrarily, Graham was well satisfied. "We should be proud," he said, "of saving two lives."

In spite of the irascibility the episode roused in me, I was chastened in retrospect. The farmers had laughed. (True, they were disguised as plumbers at the time, but as Ira Allen long ago had written of the people of Vermont, "they are all farmers.") They were right to laugh—by their lights. So, too, was Graham right to defy me, and so was I to yield. It was a clash of conditionings. What was a scandal to the plumbers and foolishness to the farmers—to paraphrase St. Paul—had its own wisdom between father and son.

Down at the far end of the stately lawn of the brick house there were two huge, beautifully shaped arbor vitae, varying the pattern of elms, maples, and pines. Beside them, from a neighboring elm branch, a high swing was rigged.

If Meredith and David were not there they were quite apt to be among the scattered pines just over the fence behind my office, engaged in the immemorial pursuit of digging to China. They made one of the best stabs at it I have ever seen, and the shaft finally had to be filled lest the cattle fall through and be converted on the other side into Fan-Gar Chow Gow-Yoke, or some other jewel of oriental cuisine.

In the warm spring rains their China project would fill up with water. Instead of ruining things for them, it gave them one of their greatest satisfactions. Suitably attired, they would sit in the flooded hole, the warm, muddy water lapping at their armpits, blissfully reading comic books.

We had known parents to be in despair over comic books and had heard portentous PTA panels on the problem. For our part, after our experience with Graham, we had ceased to worry about them. In the Nyack days he had been the biggest comic-book hoarder and wheeler-dealer in the East. His accumulations rivaled the mounds built up by eccentric recluses who die amid mountain ranges of old papers and make headlines. He traded and swapped in a radius of miles. Then it all passed and we never saw his like again. We had learned that the serious problem of the comics lies in the cultural level that offers nothing else. In the long haul, in a home with good books, the comic book can't compete.

When autumn came and the boys went to school, Meredith was desolate. We were living down in the blockhouse by then. Graham and David would set out around quarter to eight each morning to trudge the long way out to the mailbox where the school bus picked them up. One morning in September, Meredith went out to play and at some indefinite time afterward, either Ann or I, who always kept an eye out for her, became aware that she wasn't anywhere in sight.

We looked around the outside of the house, in the horse barn and in the neighborhood of the piggery—even in the cow barn, although it was off limits if she was by herself. Then we went up to the brick house, for it was common for her to go up there, though she was supposed to let us know. Not a sign. Then we thought of the pond with a sudden, frightening shock. We rushed down there and went all around its edges, searching for signs in or out of the water. We saw no trace of her but our nervous fear was not quieted. Just about then our neighbors the Stalkers telephoned Virginia to say Meredith was at their place. They had spotted her marching determinedly along the road, and corralled her for us. She was trying to follow the boys. When they asked her where she was bound she announced firmly, "I'm going to school." We scolded tolerantly, but later more severely, for it happened a few more times before she was reconciled to their daily disappearance.

The bus dropped them off again at the mailbox in the late afternoon. Nothing showed forth the different temperaments of the two boys more clearly than the contrast in their return to the house. Unfailingly Graham strode briskly all the way as if he were a Roman legionary on forced march in the Gallic wars.

At first we used to say, "Where is David?" or, "Why don't you wait for your brother?" Graham would snort impatiently and say, "Oh, he's just fooling along."

David was a natural Whitmanesque saunterer, one to loaf and invite his soul. Autumn, winter, or spring, in rain, snow, or fair weather, he would poke and dawdle along, peeping and botanizing, pausing to watch a spider at work or a procession of ants; stamping on ripe puffballs to see them explode in brown smoke; smelling things, collecting things, observing, reflecting, dreaming.

For all his comprehensive interest in nature David nurtured one phobia—snakes; this notwithstanding the fact that there were absolutely no poisonous ones in the area. There were garter snakes, good-sized blacksnakes, and one familiar denizen, a large milk snake which we saw often, and which covered a lot of ground but made its home under the barn. We taught the children that harmless snakes were useful. The milk snake helped the cats work on the mouse patrol.

The following is a pure Davidism. I cannot vouch for it beyond the fact that to this day he asserts it vehemently as one of his sharpest memories of Hand's Cove. He long cherished a characteristic David-like project of walking backward down the clay road from the brick house to the blockhouse. It was something his spirit craved but he was restrained by an overriding fear that he might step on a snake, as if these creatures, chiefly seen around the barn, were as common as in pre-Patrick Ireland.

According to David, on a certain rainy spring day, when he was clad in raincoat and boots, he screwed his courage to the sticking point and determined that this was the moment to carry out his feat. He backed along the driveway from the brick house, around the corner and down the hill. He was scared stiff at the start, but felt a resolute confidence by the time he made the turn and started down. Midway in the descent all fears had fallen away and he felt cocky to the point of childish hubris. Then he stepped on what he thought was a stick until the stick began to squirm and strike him vigorously about his booted leg. It was his old foe, the milk snake, as if this meeting had been as preordained as Oedipus' encounter with his father at the triple crossroads. Certainly, for David it was the fulfillment of his most horrid expectations. Perhaps it was for the snake, too, whose thought of crossing the road may have been haunted by the dread of being stepped on by a small boy walking backward in the rain.

In the autumn Graham and David completed a vast project that was like a parody of the wild-rice harvesting that we never carried through. Graham had thought it out in detail and exercised a martinet's control over every step. It was the great cattail harvesting. They went down repeatedly to inspect the wealth of cattails at the inner reaches of the cove. Graham would crumble one and roll it between his palms judiciously, as he'd seen farmers do with oats, then announce, "They're not ripe yet."

After several such inspections the deep-brown tails had ripened enough so that they crumbled easily into a grayish fuzz. Graham pronounced them ready, but made a strict distinction among variant strains, ruling out certain ones David started to gather, saying, "They're not the ones." When it was established which were proper they set about the harvest, breaking off the tops and filling burlap grain sacks with the ripe tails.

Back at the barn they threshed them by beating the sacks furiously against the beams in the hayloft. The stalks were then taken out and thrown away, leaving two bagfuls of pure cattail fuzz. Graham insisted that it had to age, so they hung the sacks from the high beams and left them.

About a month later the product was pronounced ready. Peeling off strips from light cardboard boxes, they rolled up fuzz-packed tubes and bound them with Scotch tape. They had produced cattail cigars. They took them a little way out in the pasture to smoke, in an abundance of fresh air. The cigars burned slowly and drew well enough, but tasted so horrible that they had to spit after each draw. Interrupted by a summons from the house, they laid their smoldering cigars on a flat rock. When they came back to them some five minutes later they were horrified. Little worms were wriggling out the ends, fleeing the fire. It was the termination of the budding industry. The infected harvest was thrown out. It was a greater deterrent from smoking than fear of cancer. As David said, they had lost confidence in the brand.

Meredith developed a penchant for bugs. I've never seen a child of either sex more venturesome in handling them. She was a busy autumnal collector of woolly-bear caterpillars. She would always attempt to forecast the coming winter weather according to the old folklore that the width of the darker band across their backs, notably wider or narrower from one year to another, foretells the mildness or severity of the season to come.

David became fascinated by butterfly collecting. We equipped him with a long-handled net and a chloroform jar. He prowled the woods and fields diligently; we often saw just the white fluttering net off in the distance. He gathered many specimens, including big luna moths captured on the windows at night, and mounted them in professional rectangular boxes of white cotton under a glass lid.

Faith, our last child, born during our final year in Vermont, never had a chance to practice a unique skill of her own on the farm, but deserves citation nevertheless. She is the world's greatest specialist in the detection and nurture of little red spiders. Later, in our home in Connecticut, we could be walking across the lawn with Faith, or even through dense woods, and she would cry out with joy, "Oh, a red spider!" Reaching down, she would come up with a creature so tiny—like unto a pinhead—that I had trouble enough seeing either its shape or its color when she held it out to me on a finger tip. She kept colonies of them in jars. In a few moments' time she could collect a dozen or so in the palm of her hand, where they looked like incipient prickly heat. She used to horrify our cleaning woman by this rashness, who warned her they would surely bite her. You might as well expect a germ to bite you.

It was ironic that Faith was a mere infant on the farm, for she developed into a splendid miniature horsewoman. She is our most diminutive child, but at twelve years old, weighing only ninety pounds, she could manage horses with confidence, cleaning their stables, picking their hooves, whopping them over the nose if they got nippy, and riding them with confidence and style—all long after we had left the one place where she could have kept a horse of her own.

Of all aspects of the children on the farm, the permanently memorable one for us is the chronicle of the Oo family. Each of our children in turn had an imaginary playmate, as almost all children do. I don't remember David's, but Graham consorted for a while with a drab, featureless couple called Mr. Meatman and Mrs. Spinach, whose own relationship was shadowy. Meredith, in the fertility of her inner life at age four to five, had three. They lived lives of such intensity that all of us were drawn into them hypnotically.

Having preserved our own sense of wonder—in short, not having grown up—Ann and I always walked with our children, not only one mile but twain, along whatever road of fantasy they compelled us to go, welcoming and befriending whomever we met on the way. These encounters were much too absorbing for any patronizing, faked interest; we were enthralled.

The first to appear was Oo, pronounced as in "Boo!" He was conventional enough, played games, had assorted misadventures and a great many sharp opinions on all subjects, generally differing notably from ours, which Meredith freely quoted in rebuttal of parental views. Then one time, seeing her deeply engrossed in some mysterious activity, I inquired amiably if she were playing with Oo.

"No," she said, "I'm playing with Other-Oo."

We were roused at once to a heightened interest. Oo and Other-Oo seemed an advanced concept, like matter and antimatter. Other-Oo had come to stay. Meredith played continually with either or both of them. Besides this active pair there was a numerous Oo family, including their parents and distant relatives.

They became such accepted features that we were unguarded and unbraced for shock on the morning many months later when Meredith announced, "Other-Oo is dead."

We were grieved. Under question, Meredith explained that she had found Other-Oo dead behind a big wing chair in the living room.

I asked, "How did he die?"

Meredith said, "From dandruff."

"Dandruff!" I repeated in alarmed astonishment. As a chronic sufferer I had hitherto deemed it annoying but not dangerous.

"Yes," she said, "he drank a bottle of dandruff, but 'cept."

Meredith used the phrase "but 'cept" in a wide range of contexts, analogous to the ubiquitous German *also*. In retrospect, years later, she said that by dandruff she meant dandruff-remover shampoo, a bottle of which was generally in my bathroom.

Later on that sad day, as I immersed myself in work to muffle the shock of the event, a Vermont writer with whom I had some professional association, dropped in unexpectedly for his first visit to our farm. This was Ralph Nading Hill, of Burlington, author of *The Winooski*, in the Rivers of America Series, and other books.

Ralph is not likely to forget that first day he spent with us. Expecting to talk literary shop, instead he found himself in a bereaved household. He sat spellbound at lunch as Meredith imparted to him the news about Other-Oo, with a brief sketch of the deceased's life and pleasant association with her. She then shocked us all further by disclosing the full scope of the disaster, having felt that we could not bear it all at once. Oo also had died, the day before, of causes unknown.

I asked whether Other-Oo might have drunk the dandruff because of grief over his brother's death.

"But 'cept," Meredith added, "the mother and father are going to die tomorrow."

So they did. Meredith confirmed it solemnly. The Oo family was wiped out and had become as the baseless fabric of a dream.

This hurt me and I asked—foolishly—if there wasn't anything that could be done about it.

"No," she insisted, with the serene acceptance of the

Preacher in Ecclesiastes, "they just had to die. It was the time."

We adjusted slowly to this gap in the household. Meredith talked frequently of both Oo and Other-Oo, in affectionate reminiscence of her adventures with them.

It was months later, after time had eased the loss, that Meredith abruptly announced that she had found Other-Oo again, behind the same chair, not dead. In cold logic I presume that if you can find somebody dead you can just as well find them not dead. After all, Stanley found Livingstone not dead and became famous for it. I had a vision of Meredith, rounding the wing chair, coming face to face with an unexpected presence, and saying with absolute composure, "Other-Oo, I presume?"

It turned out that the entire Oo family was back, without further fanfare or explanation. We told Meredith we were awfully happy about it. She agreed calmly that it was indeed fortunate. None of us were disposed to look this gift horse in the mouth.

Not long after that, her third companion appeared. I don't know how many other parents have been confronted by their children with a possibly undesirable or slightly sinister imaginary playmate, but this one was disquieting.

His name was Indian Power. We have no inkling of his origin or inspiration. He sprang full-panoplied from Meredith's brow—and he had a formidable panoply.

She explained that Indian Power was an old friend of Oo and Other-Oo. "But 'cept you can't trust him," she added darkly. "He has a knife."

She never forgot that attribute. The relationship was provocatively tense and wary. Once, having sat silently for a while on the edge of an adult conversation, she heard the word "trust." Meredith sprang up and stopped the conversation cold by asserting, "You can't trust Indian Power! He has a sign in his house that says, 'You can't trust me!' "

The Oo boys and Indian Power roved about the whole state of Vermont quite restlessly during a period when I was doing the same on professional errands. We would be driving along the road and Meredith would point suddenly to a house and say, "That's where Oo lives now" or "That's Indian Power's house." They were part of our family life for a couple of years and were Meredith's models for methods and behavior. "The way Other-Oo . . ." she would begin, or "What Indian Power always does . . ."

But paths diverge; a sad circumstance in most of our friendships. When Meredith went to school the lines of communication became faint with Oo, Other-Oo, and Indian Power. They settled down from their restless quests. Oo and Other-Oo took a little white tenant house on a farm just outside Middlebury. They live there to this day, unless Other-Oo has taken to dandruff drinking again. Indian Power lives near by in a handsome brick house. Meredith's last report of record was that he was engaged in making and selling Christmas wreaths and cutting down trees.

As David said reflectively, "It's a good job for him."

CRAXO

CHAPTER FIFTEEN

Fencing Without Foils

ROBERT FROST SAID, "Good fences make good neighbors."
What's more, they make good farmers—or perhaps good
farmers make good fences. Apart from the subtle, psychological symbols of privacy and individuality that "fences" mean
to Frost, a fence may be only a boundary to an orchardist or a
truck farmer, but for the dairy farmer it is essential.

First of all there is the barnyard. In our case, as in many, it
was enclosed with a wooden plank fence, somewhat like a
horse fence but red instead of white. This is fine so long as
the wood is not rotten and the posts are firm. A weak and
leaning barnyard fence means trouble, for the cattle will mill
around the yard in their winter drinking and exercise periods.
They'll bump against the fence, rub against it for the relief of
barn itch, and perhaps try to climb over it when they are in
heat. A barnyard also must have two or three good wide
gates, big enough for a truck to drive through, and the posts
must be straight and firm so that the gates will swing.

Since the picturesque rail fence has become an expensive, decorative luxury, the basic farm fence is barbed wire. Four-strand fence is best, which means a lot of wire and a lot of barbs. It also means a lot of posts, which means a lot of post holes.

It is a general truth that when a farm has begun to run down, as ours had, through a long lack of effective resident-owner management, one of the early symptoms is sagging fences. This was one of the first matters we had to consider. What's more, we required sheep fencing, too, which is of wire net with relatively small holes. Fortunately, because of the farm's history of sheep, an adequate fence existed in the small meadow where Virginia's few sheep were confined. We had only minimal maintenance to do for that.

What first caught us in the toils of fencing was our natural emotional-intellectual commitment to conservation. The county forester, a robust, ruddy, handsome, genial man named Art Heitman, walked with us through our several wooded areas and pointed out the depredations of cattle. Their place is pasture. They have no business in woods or groves. The forester showed us the scarred or broken roots exposed by hooves. They would trip the unwary walker, but the real concern was that they were the gateway to tree disease, the source of heart rot, and a diminution of nourishment and water for the tree. Fine maples, oaks, and pines alike were declining from such abuse, and numerous large dead-stick trees, some standing, others partially or wholly fallen, were the results of cattle grazing where they should not be.

The boys and I cut down a lot of those standing dead trees scattered about the rim of the pasture, in which woodpeckers had hollowed out monstrous holes. The standing ones were still dry and burnable. At the same time, as we knew, they are

[171]

the most dangerous kind of tree to fell. Tenacious wood fibers have dried out and lost their strength; as you saw or chop, the weakening tree will not give way gradually but snap off abruptly, with no warning. We worked cautiously and had a few scares but were lucky to have no mishaps.

Another impressive phase of the forester's demonstration, especially in our beautiful stands of sugar maples, was the fact that no prosperous young regrowth of trees was coming along to replace the old generations. Cattle liked nothing better than to vary their grass diet with succulent young sprouting trees.

"Get the cattle out of here," the forester promised, "and in a year or so you'll see a wealth of young trees springing up that you can thin out selectively."

Sadly enough, all but a minority of the very best farmers, chiefly the younger men who had been to the agricultural school, were indifferent to their wood lots, as long as it looked as though there would be plenty to cut for the short period they could see ahead. Some farmers would sell off their woods and allow them to be clear-cut for a small but quick return, and take no step to reforest again. As for taking the time and spending the money to fence extensively—it was out of the question.

For all our grasp of the principle involved, we could not afford to put up many thousands of feet of strong fence— barbed wire, rail, or whatever. This was no new problem to the foresters—a breed of men conditioned by their work to be generally pessimistic, yet to keep alive faint glimmers of hope. They offered a suggestion: an electric fence.

The only electric fences I knew anything about at that time were those high-voltage ones of concentration camps. The only application of such fences that I could imagine in

Vermont would be a desperate man's quest for a solution to the problem of keeping transient hired hands.

Gently the foresters explained to me the mysteries of the six-volt electric fence. It can be strung on almost any kind of post, as heavy or light as seems expedient and practical. The wire—a smooth, fairly heavy-gauge steel or copper—must not touch the posts or anything that will ground it. It is run through porcelain insulators nailed to the posts, on the interior side of the enclosed area. At one end of the line is the control box, or pulsator. It is powered by six-volt dry-cell batteries. There is an oscillating circuit breaker that clicks back and forth with a metronomic swing and sends a pulse of power through the line about every two seconds.

Any creature that touches the line will ground it and get a repeated, harmless, but unpleasant shock as long as he maintains contact. I say unpleasant because I found it distinctly so. Electric shocks sicken me by seeming to make my heart flip over, and have thus served me as an effective deterrent to capital crimes. Unfortunately the only way to know whether the fence was working or not was to grab it and find out. I had to tolerate it. Some people did not mind holding on to it indefinitely. The boys didn't object much and used to egg Meredith on to grab it. The longer the line, the weaker the shock; the damper the ground, the stronger. Sticks falling across the line would ground it slightly and weaken if not kill it.

The important thing was that farm creatures did not like it. Any normal cow brushing against it, or touching it experimentally with her nose, would shy back. Such a fence can be strung at appropriately lower heights for pigs, who do not like it one bit.

These fences are most effective for small enclosures, for

short periods of time, and to confine docile beasts. Our electric fence was so vast that it seemed like a rural electrification
project; it was expected to work a long time and to confine
unruly creatures. It was what David might have called "pesti-
mum" rather than optimum circumstances. But we tried, we
always tried.

In fact, we had two fences. The smaller, which even then
was a matter of a good half-mile or more, completely enclosed
the sugarbush in the extreme southeast sector of the farm.
Because there were relatively fewer cattle there it gave us the
least problems, though it must not be thought it gave us
none. It skirted a part of the ten acres that drained into the
pond. We never let anyone but Susan or some other of our
own creatures into it. Though not a bad pasture, it contained
a good bit of a tough, thin-leafed sheep grass which the cows
did not like.

The other fence line needs further explanation, for it was
intended to protect more than woods. I mentioned during
the account of our water problems how relentlessly Lake
Champlain erodes its banks wherever they are not rock ledge.
Trees slow the process, though they do not halt it. It was an
impressive experience to walk the whole length of the north
side of the great point. It fell off steeply some twenty feet or
more in crumbling clay precipices and slopes. Deeper bites
had sunk in at certain places, forming miniature clay fjords, so
that to walk the edge of the promontory required one to follow an irregular, saw-tooth course. In one of those gullies lay
a charming, curved-runnered, red-painted Victorian sleigh,
from the days when, as Nathan Hand's relative had written
so long ago, "ye people" were "continually slaying backwards
& forwards." From the end of the point jutting far into the
lake, back along the north side, was a distance of a half-mile

or more, and the line of shore then swung north, shortly becoming wooded, and at last stony.

In the high-water seasons the lake nibbled steadily at the
base. During the summer the level receded by twenty to
thirty feet, leaving clay shallows. One could wade in them,
knee-deep in the pale-gray clay, which would suck and cling
but was just hard enough not to degenerate into quicksand.
The lake was no good for swimming or boat launching at
such places. The clay was good for sculpture and ceramic use,
and for a long time we had rough clay ashtrays, merely sun-
baked, that the children made and occasionally tried to sell to
visitors. One would find natural clay objects along the shore,
water-shaped and sun-baked, resembling the abstract forms in
space of Arp and other modern sculptors.

There was a good deal more land on that promontory in
the days of Samuel Herrick and Nathan Hand. There will be
much less before Lake Champlain has disappeared in a distant future. It is only the inexorable diminishment of the lake
itself—a slow but continual process ever since the great gla-
cier that made it retreated—that keeps me from predicting
the ultimate total disappearance of the promontory.

I found in the Hand letters that Augustus C. Hand, who
lived in Elizabethtown, New York, had passed down the lake
by water in June of 1861, and afterward reported in a letter
to his sisters, who lived on the farm: "Passed Hand's place
on Saturday, and Oh, how the *point* is worn off. We must
protect it. Drive down Piles! or slabs and try to get a growth
of willows. How foolish we have been. Real estate is all we
have left in this country and the only property that is safe if
any. And $50. would probably have done wonders towards
preservation."

Some ninety years later, with the attrition more advanced,

we felt the full fervor of that early Augustus Hand. The forester wanted us to protect the northern tract of woods. Allen Mayville of the U.S. Soil Conservation office wanted us to protect the point. Our hearts beat with the zeal to do both.

The electric fence was to be the first step. We thought of it as sweeping boldly in a vast curve from the absolute tip of the point, running as close to the north edge of the crumbling bank as the deep inroads would permit, then up and around the woods and thus along their eastern border all the way to the northern limit of the property. It used up over a mile and a half of wire.

We tackled that fence project in the very first summer, and how we toiled at it! Graham and I did most of it, but Frank, the boy who worked for Virginia that season, bore a hand. Herbert Michelman and others among our friends who came to stay at Virginia's pitched in. David and Ann helped out with wire stringing and the hammering-on of insulators. We used posts of varying sizes, as the character of the ground dictated. For the larger ones I bought and learned to use a post-hole digger, an instrument rather like a man-sized corkscrew, which was fun to use if the ground wasn't stony. Well-equipped farmers have power diggers attached to tractors.

We found quickly that the fence was much too long for a single pulsator unit, so we put in a second battery box midway. Also, there was another complication. Good practice called for the rotating of pastures. We had two principal pasture areas—the one down on the promontory and the other in the northeast upland. We wanted to make a corridor that could be cut off, along which cattle could be moved from one large area to the other. The electric fence would form one side of this passageway. The other, bordering on our richest alfalfa hay meadow, was to be an extension of the barbed-wire fence that already protected part of that valuable and tempting area.

For the stretch of barbed-wire fence—four-strand—I needed professional help. Dan, one of the farmers with whom we had our hay and cattle dealings, came down to help me do it, or more accurately, to do it with my help. The first phase of that help I found hair-raising. We dug post holes, set in the posts, and then Dan pounded them in firmly with a sixteen-pound maul. He would be standing up on a wagon bed. I would be down on the ground, holding the post upright in its hole. Dan would swing that mighty hammer back over his head and belt it down on the post with a shock that would travel up my arms and down my spine into the ground through both my feet. He never missed a stroke, but I never missed an anguished anticipation of what would happen to me if he did.

The stringing of the barbed wire was a venture, too. It is best done in the heaviest of leather work gloves, for it is vicious stuff, likely to bite you now and then in spite of the utmost care. There are divers tools and jacks for tightening the wire to a true singing tautness—a process which is also the test of well-set posts, for otherwise you can pop a post out like a cork while tightening the wire. To break the wire, and have it lash back at you also, is a nasty thing. Good braced corner posts are the key to taut fencing.

One tool I still cherish from this labor is that magnificent basic instrument: fencing pliers. They are so versatile that I still use them for many things. They are long-handled and heavy. One side of their curved head is a narrow, ridged hammer face, for driving in the fence staples that hold the wire to the posts. The opposite side terminates in a miniature anvil beak, which is for prying out staples. In the center of the top, opening or closing with the movement of the handles, is a two-sectioned opening that will pull anything, from an ordinary nail to a spike. On each side, below the top, is a strong wire cutter, and in the crotch of the handle, another toothed grip for wrenching or drawing nails or spikes, or squeezing, twisting, or braiding wire. It is a satisfying instrument, so well designed as to be esthetic, too. Even one as clumsy with tools as I am can do a great deal with it.

As for our electric fence, it was too long. The most I can say is that because of it, the cattle were slightly less often out of bounds than if it hadn't been there at all—but of itself it was inadequate to keep them out. Irrepressible, unpenned young stock would move against it, single file or in battalions, and have it down before they had time to react to the shock. Sometimes the shock wasn't there. Over that vast stretch the possibilities for interruptions in the circuit were immense and varied. It deterred chiefly in that the cattle had other options than going through the wire, which they exercised a good deal of the time. But we coddled and patrolled that fence constantly. It was a regular daily assignment for one of the boys to test it for shock and to patrol it, clearing it of grounding impediments, or repairing it if the interruption was not major. Posts constantly had to be reset, the line spliced, the batteries replaced.

The tip of the point quickly showed us the first great problem. The line ran to the water's edge in early summer, but the water receded. The line had to be lengthened steadily to keep up with that. But then the cattle would wade out into the shallows and get around the end of the fence. Being then on the wrong side, they would either break back out somewhere, or with perverse docility accept being penned precisely where we didn't want them. It was a question of who was fencing in whom.

Graham and I were forced to labor at running a three-strand line of barbed wire thirty feet or so out into the shallow water at the end of the point, sinking long poles in the clay to hold it. Sometimes that would keel over without the aid of cattle; a high wind would whip up a surf on the lake and we'd have to go down and set the posts up again.

It became a family syndrome to look out the living-room windows of the blockhouse, down toward the point, and cry out, "The heifers are through the fence again!" Whereupon down we would trot, the long way, to herd out the beasts and repair the fence.

One afternoon at dusk, just as Graham and I were starting to trek back from the end of the point, we saw a sight we will never forget. We spotted it simultaneously. A brilliant meteoric fireball was coming at us from the east, right over the line of the houses, on a trajectory that first looked as if we were the target. It gave the illusion of coming very slowly and being close over our heads, and it was silent—facts which obviously mean that it was high indeed. As it passed right above us it looked the size of a bowling ball and was disintegrating into a flaming tail. We turned as it went over us, and above the lake it exploded into fragments and disappeared in a ghostly silence. We were exhilarated and awed and talked of it for days.

Now, it had never been conceived that this vexing electric fence was to be a permanent installation. My early letters in the first summer's euphoria had looked ahead to plantings. Allen Mayville and Art Heitman said that along the line of the fence we should plant multiflora rose, a hardy, blossoming, thorny plant that would grow up from small shoots and in five or six years be over our heads and intertwined into a stout, thorny barrier worthy of the Sleeping Beauty. It would be a natural permanent fence. The government would give us all the multiflora rose—some four thousand plants—and Allen and Art would help us put it in.

We worked for days and days at this task. I thought it should be planted on the side of the fence away from the cattle—*sometimes* away, depending on which side the cattle chose to dwell, from time to time. Allen said not so. Multiflora rose was so hardy that the more we walked on it, the more cattle tramped on it, the more dense and tangled it would grow. We heeled in the slender but prickly little sprigs in long narrow trenches turned over by plow. Heeling meant literally that you poked a little hole, stuck in the shoot, and kicked the plant savagely with your heel to tramp it down. Then, to our mild horror, Allen proceeded to drive up and down the row with the wheels of his pickup truck to pack the plants in harder. Not only would the hedge be a great help when it got its growth, we were assured, but it would also be a thing of blossoming beauty every spring.

Still, that was not all. It was intended that we should plant Norway spruce, white pine, and black-locust trees, row upon row, to a depth of a hundred feet back from the edge of the north side of the point, and that we should plant a multiplicity of big-rooted, fast-growing, tenacious shrubs in the crumbling banks of clay. These included willow whips and silky cornel, a hardwood shrub loosely related to the dogwood family, Tartarian honeysuckle, filbert, coralberry and high-bush cranberry. Augustus Hand had been knowledgeable when he spoke of willows in 1861.

There were several steps to putting in these and it was accomplished in April of 1949, when we had been on the farm about a year. First of all, on April 5 the boys and I set out with Allen Mayville and three farmer's sons who were friends of Graham's, some of us in a light truck and some in Art Heitman's car, to spend the day cutting willow whips.

It was a long jaunt, for we were to cut the willows along the edges of the Winooski River (the name means Onion River), east of Burlington, seventy-five miles away. The day was extraordinarily beautiful—balmy, fragrant, cloudless. On the great panoramic perspectives of the lake, as one drives toward Burlington, the waters were of exceptionally deep azure. Whiteface and its neighboring Adirondack peaks westward, and the Camel's Hump and Mount Mansfield in the Green Mountains, still wore their crowns of snow. I was peacefully high-hearted, partly for the good thing we were doing, but chiefly because Ann was home from the hospital, barely a few days, by grace and mercy, from a surgical crisis that had all but taken her life. Bliss was it in that day to be alive.

The Winooski valley is full of lovely haunts and mountain-shadowed gorges. The government men took us to a place where the green willows grew in profusion. These were not trees, of course, but osiers, the wicker or basket willows that will grow rank and strong and weave their roots below ground as basket weavers will do with their tops. We all had a wonderful time, working, picnicking, and working again. In several hours we cut upward of five thousand willow whips that would root themselves quickly upon being thrust in the ground. We packed them in the truck, tied in great bundles. Back home, we carried the bundles to the edge of the pond and laid them half their length in water. It not only kept them fresh and alive, but by the time they were moved for planting a week later they had already begun to sprout.

That was a Tuesday. The following Monday, Art and Allen

came with a thousand young white pines, a thousand Norway spruce, and a thousand black-locust trees, which the forestry service was giving us. They were driven down across the pasture and unloaded in clumps. At the same time a tractor was plowing rows of furrows to facilitate the setting-in of the trees.

The next day, the twelfth, which was the Tuesday in Holy Week, was as supernally beautiful as the time of our willow cutting had been. Countless hands were needed. Allen and Art considered this a major conservation demonstration in the public interest. They had arranged to bring several busloads of boys and girls all the way from the Middlebury High School and the small school in the village. The Middlebury principal and several teachers came. There were over a hundred people at the farm, in all. Lucien Pacquette, the county agent, came too. Reporters were there, and photographers, from Burlington and Rutland papers which ran articles and pictures about the project the next day.

We took Ann down to the promontory to see the fun. Under the skillful direction of the government men, dividing up the specialized tasks, row upon row of trees were set in. Thousands of shrubs were planted in the raw clay bank; some, like the willows, were just thrust in. Others required a preparatory jab with a planting tool to create a hole for them. I worked at that with the boys, some of us in bare feet caked with the sticky clay that pulled boots off many. Everyone had brought lunch, and we carried down milk cans of lemonade, milk, and water. The work had begun at nine o'clock in the morning and was finished by two in the afternoon. There are not many days of my life that I have considered better spent; there have been few when I felt happier or closer to the world that nurtures me. It was something that captured us all, with a heady joy and companionship.

We thought a great deal of those agricultural agents, conservation men, and foresters. They are a good breed, pursuing a wholesome work. Forestry appealed to me particularly and I'd have been happy to see a son take up the work. They practice a far-ranging, disinterested husbandry of our earth, resisting the spoilers, so that all of us, even those fast-pent in cities, owe them more than we dream. They keep our forests and woods from wanton spoliation, reforest denuded or waste ground, preserve beauty and conserve water—which also helps to diminish floods and erosion. The city dweller enjoys these benefits when he fares afield, but indirectly they aid his pocketbook when he bides at home, in prices of food, lumber products, and the general care of national resources in natural wealth.

There are county, state, and federal foresters. In our years in Vermont we co-operated with them in every way we could, going to meetings, sitting on discussion panels, and the like. We became friends with the U. S. forester, a man appropriately named Bush, who was in charge of the National Forest tracts in the Green Mountains. The boys and I spent a long-remembered day with him one spring, touring all his preserve, including the few precious areas of virgin forest left there, and seeing also where supervised timber harvesting was being done.

CHAPTER SIXTEEN

The Thundering Herd

THE ACTION BEGAN on a Sunday at the end of July. Dan had several expectant Holstein heifers summering in our pastures. I kept an eye on them, as they drifted about, to give him word when the calves were dropped. On a late afternoon I was coming up from the lake where I had helped some friends, staying at Virginia's, to launch my rowboat fitted with their outboard motor. On my way across the pasture I saw three new calves amidst a huddle of heifers.

I called Dan and he came down with a truck and two men, named Leon and Bill. The four of us went down in the pasture toward the point. Unlike lone and simple Susan who had let us come and get her first calf, long ago, these heifers of Dan's were a wild bunch. In a sense they were organized, too, for every group of cow-critters politics until it finds a queen, and her whim is herd law. The queen of this small herd, which had been months together on open range without being handled, was a hefty white heifer, the mother of one of the new calves. The group saw us coming from afar and took off in cautious evasive action—the calves wobbling along.

We fanned out in an encircling tactic. Perceiving this, as we moved in, the heifers bolted in earnest, stormed through our thin red line, and surged up the corridor toward the barn. This passage from one large pasture area to another was bordered on the south by the four-strand barbed-wire fence Dan and I had constructed, and on the north by the mild deterrent of my electric fence. At the queen's whim the heifers veered sharply north, swept through the electric fence, snapping the wire and upsetting a half-dozen of my posts, and vanished into the woods in the general direction of the camp and the rock ledges along the lake.

The calves had been abandoned and wobbled forlornly about as we surrounded them.

"We'll have to take 'em in," Dan said. "It may bring back the others."

We corralled the little creatures and guided them in the way they should go. It was a long uphill trek to the barnyard. By the time we got them there and lifted them onto the truck it was late. We scanned the northerly horizon. There was no trace of the heifers. Dan could wait no longer. He departed, planning to come the next day and give chase. I went out to do about an hour's work on the electric fence. This was mere prologue to what we remember as the three-day heifer chase.

Ann and I awakened the next morning to a sound of clumping and shuffling. About a dozen heifers were milling around our yard, kicking up divots on the lawn and breaking our young trees and bushes. The queen and the other two recent mothers were looking for the calves. We didn't know how this bunch had got there. I had to go to the barn, and I thought that I would open the big gate and that Ann would then come out the rear door of the blockhouse and we could try to shunt them inside the inviting barnyard.

I carried out my move and threw out some fresh hay as a possible inducement. But as Ann quietly approached them from the other side, the white queen suddenly gave a leap and a snort and the heifers streamed up the road toward the brick house, thundered across its lawn, and disappeared behind the building. We could see Virginia emerge from the brick house gesticulating at the stampede.

They had crashed through the small old gate in the fence between the sheep barn and the tool shed, snapping off one of its posts. Now they were back on the north pasture, close to the edge of the woods.

Dan and his men came down around midday. By this time the heifer band had drifted up to the northeast corner into the hickory grove. Ann, the boys, and I joined the expedition, so that there were seven of us in the field. Our stratagem was to avoid another panic rush by flanking them, almost unbeknownst to ourselves. We approached from various directions, strolling casually, stopping, and appearing to be bent on other errands. The heifers shifted nervously. We wanted to make them drift gradually southwest, toward the barnyard. Instead, they moved gingerly straight west. When this course brought them near the woods Dan's men moved more decisively to keep them out of the trees. Instantly they were off, dashed south, nearly bowling the boys off their feet, flanked us widely, and vanished into the woods in spite of all our efforts.

We began to prowl the woods in a confused parody of the wilderness campaign around Richmond. Some critters had slithered down the steep bank onto the rocky shore, at risk of limb. We had to concentrate on getting them back up the banks, amid small avalanches of slate. Roaming, shouting, and bush beating, we got them back to the edge of the woods in time, approaching the upper neck of the corridor that led down to the pasture on the point.

Dan dispatched three men to circle around and take up a stance in that corridor just below the latitude of the barn, to turn the herd if they tried to go down to the point. The rest of us again began to urge them in the direction of the yard. David was sent around to open the rear gate of the barnyard, and make sure that all its other gates were secure.

The heifers moved slowly for a few moments in the general direction desired, and our hopes rose. Then for no discernible reason the devil entered them again. They began to run; we ran to keep up; they swerved west into the corridor toward the point. We shouted. The men who had gone to block that way shouted in response and advanced toward us. The heifers didn't miss a stride. They swerved again, following their demoniac white queen, and the whole bunch ran through the four-strand barbed-wire fence as if it didn't exist. I wouldn't have believed it if I hadn't seen it.

The lead heifers must have been torn and scratched savagely. Three posts were out and twisted crazily in a barbed-wire entanglement; two more were leaning far over. The top strand was snapped, the rest were sprung and pushed over. The weight and velocity of the wild heifers had simply overrun the fence. Dan ran up, cursing sulphurously.

Now the worst had happened. The heifers had scattered. The white leader and a couple or so of others had dashed off across the alfalfa meadow toward the cove. We saw some galloping up the road, vanishing from sight over the crest. A couple more had gone off tangentially around the pond dam. Two had given up and were standing quite docilely in front of the blockhouse. The baleful influence of leadership was removed. Their flanks were scratched nastily from the debacle at the fence; they were tired and ready to go. One of them was a freshened heifer. Glumly Dan and his men drove these up the ramp into the truck, looking as if their true mood was to take no prisoners alive.

They drove off, and the morning and the evening were the first day—except not quite for us. When milking time came I discovered that all our own little herd was gone. The spectacular, fence-crashing flight had made everyone forget that the back gate to the barnyard had been opened. The boys and I fared forth again, hoping the virus of revolution had not infected our docile kine. We found them way up at the north end. They were obedient enough about coming back, except for innocent frisks, but it was late and dark before chores were done that night.

The next day was Tuesday. To start it off, Dan and his men came down and helped me fix the fence. One more heifer wandered in and gave herself up—another of the freshened ones, the only mother left at large being the demoniac white heifer who seemed bent on becoming a legend in her lifetime. Still another heifer was reported in an apple orchard and Dan caught her there.

We began to search again. I was developing fevered fantasies by this time, and driving back and forth from the village for the mail, I was tempted to bellow to every passing vehicle, like Ahab, "Ahoy! Have ye seen the White Heifer?"

This day we searched the cove and at last flushed out the white one and two others. They retreated into the narrowing cove until it became marshy. The white one waded out to the depth of her belly and glowered at us. I longed for a harpoon. The other two surrendered. The prudent thing was to make sure of the two in hand, so we drove them the long way back to the barn and waiting truck, with no difficulty once the spell of evil companionship was lifted.

Ann reported a phone call from the Marceau farm with word that a strange heifer had wandered in with their milking herd. We proceeded there and found penned in their barnyard one of the truants who must have ranked second in command. She fought like a fiend against going up the ramp into the truck. The men got ropes on her to keep her from breaking clear again. She bucked and kicked and braced her feet. It took a man clutching the ropes at either side of her head and the jabbing tines of a manure fork at her rear to work her into the truck.

The boys and I were so involved that we followed in our car to Dan's farm. There the unloading was as rough a process as the loading had been. In the infectious excitement Dan's tethered bull pulled up his stake, and a diversionary action had to be launched to recapture him. He proved not half so tough a customer as the young females.

Dan reported that all were accounted for except the white heifer, the mastermind of the mutiny. Wednesday morning, the third day, we saw the quarry down in a corner of the alfalfa meadow. Dan, Leon, and Bill arrived once more with the big truck and a pickup. They looked over the situation again and then launched the maddest phase of the whole operation, having reached an approximate point of not giving a damn for life, limb, or property, plus a certain steam-venting zest of their own.

The meadow had been mowed not long before, so was passable though bumpy. Dan drove the pickup truck. Bill rode its running board, hanging on with one arm through the window, a rope with a lasso loop in his other hand. We stood up by the barnyard and watched the rodeo.

Leon skirted around on foot and drove the heifer out into the open ground. Dan began to circle her widely with the pickup truck, driving the heifer to the center of the meadow, careening wildly over bumps and chuck holes. Bill, uttering cowboy yips, clung on magically and swung his rope. They were forcing the heifer to circle in an ever-tighter orbit until Bill was able to toss his loop of rope over her head. Dan slammed on his brakes; Bill leaped off; Leon closed in. The heifer strained at the rope, put up a face-saving tussle, then surrendered unconditionally. The truth was, she was ready to go—her subjects were gone and she needed milking desperately.

We watched the truck vanish over our hill with the captive barbarian princess. So ended three days of ignominy—the revolt of the critters.

It was not our first experience of such orneriness. Bovine females generally are placid and docile once they are matronly cows in the regimen of a dairy herd. Yearling to two-year heifers can be a bumptious lot when they run at large, full of infinite curiosity and adolescent wild spirits.

Graham and I had discovered this the second winter on the farm. This time our heat-source boarders were thirteen Holstein heifers of Ollie Farnham's. When we drove them in after the evening watering they would throw their heavy weight wildly about the barn, charging up the aisles, milling about and utterly refusing to put their heads through the stanchions.

We tried the tactic of putting down a small heap of oats in

the trough inside their stanchions. The heifers would detect it and poke their heads through to eat. But the moment one of us attempted to approach to slide up the board to close the stanchion, the heifer would back out immediately, and so would her neighbors. Night after night it took us an intolerable time to get them penned.

At this point Graham rose to one of his finest hours. Patiently he gathered up a collection of the heavy twine from hay bales. He knotted together a great length of them and looped them in tandem from one to another of the sliding bars of the stanchions. It took him the better part of an afternoon to perfect his plan. When I showed up for the evening milking, the cattle were still in the yard and Graham was there, too.

"You watch what it's going to be like tonight, Daddy."

We took in our own group first, as usual. Then came the obstreperous thirteen. Graham had distributed the grain. The heifers dived into the stanchions to eat it, watching warily but satisfied that we were well away from them up at the end of the barn. Graham seized the end of his cord and yanked it. Clacking in unison, thirteen stanchions closed smartly on thirteen astonished heifers. Graham was triumphantly and justly proud of what he called his cow trap. With minor repairs it served us well through the whole winter.

CHAPTER SEVENTEEN

A Series of Cat-astrophes

THE SAME DAY that we got the pigs from the Aunchman, David noticed a young tortoise-shell cat among a vast feline tribe around the house. He asked if he might have her and was told to help himself. Ann and I consented, having a job available for a cat at the moment.

David named her Calico. He would sit in a big old rocking chair, a beaming tow-headed figure, with the cat curled up on his lap and enjoying the ride. "Calico is the most beautiful cat in the world," he asserted over and over. She was not only beautiful, she took her responsibilities seriously and was a first-rate mouser and ratter; in the words of Eliot's Old Possum, she was eminently a practical cat. Though she poked around the barns a good deal, she was our official house cat. There were to be many others on the farm but Calico, gentle and affectionate, was always David's special pet.

Calico was also a hardy hiking cat. One biting January day

Ann and I took a long walk down the fields and across the cove on the ice to explore the otherwise inaccessible woods on the other side. Calico accompanied us all the way, as did our German shepherd dog, with whom she had established certain firm understandings. She picked her way across the ice with delicate tread, her distaste for the surface clear in each flick of her feet, but she would not abandon the party.

Virginia had acquired a mottled gray cat of peculiar temperament whom she called Twinkle. On Meredith's tongue in those early days the name came out "Drickle." This pleased us all, especially Graham, and before long it became the cat's permanent name, far more appropriate to his eccentric nature. Drickle had six or seven toes on each foot, which gave him the appearance of walking on feet borrowed from some larger animal. Nervous and irascible by nature, he would scratch or bite as soon as look at you, out of sheer perversity. Graham was amused by the preposterous creature's cantankerousness and held him in cautious esteem. For some reason Drickle liked me as much as he was capable of liking anybody, possibly because of buried affinities of character. Sometimes when I walked from my office down to the blockhouse Drickle would spring up my back, sinking in his claws as if I were a tree trunk, perch precariously on my shoulder, and ride down, from time to time giving me a random scratch or bite along the way to caution me against any nonsense.

Cats began to pop up anywhere. Early in the first winter we became aware of a group of kittens living under the cattle barn—the offspring of some stray, for Calico was still chaste. They were wild and wary, vanishing instantly at the remotest approach. We got only distant glimpses of them. Once in a while we caught sight of their nondescript mother but she ceased to show up after a while. Since there were sacks of feed grain in the barn, the mice and rats were plentiful; there were jobs for all and we accepted the furtive presence of the cats.

As I milked Susan, twice daily, one of the kittens began to put in a cautious appearance in the barn. He was jet-black, yellow-eyed, consumed with curiosity and an obvious longing to be adopted—the only one in his family with such an urge. I chirped at him encouragingly but his approaches were very gradual. It was only after days of his tentative scouting that he let me touch him lightly at arm's length.

Then abruptly his courage picked up. He appeared for every milking, would sit on his haunches beside me and squall brashly for milk. I did the trick I had seen farmers do with cats in their barns, and squirted a stream of milk right at him. The kitten grasped the idea quickly. He would open his pink mouth wide and receive the warm jet with much splattering, then patiently lick himself dry.

I called him Blackie and began to give him his own small saucer of milk morning and evening. At night he curled up by Susan or the calves for warmth—bucolically touching, but hazardous. I was much attached to him, but before ever he grew up I was grieved one morning to find him as flat and stiff as a gingerbread cookie. Susan had rolled over on him in the night.

In the fullness of time Calico found love somewhere and had her own first litter of kittens. Ann and I were awakened at four o'clock one morning by the sound of the kittens being born in our bedroom. We got Graham and David up to see them. All went back to bed at last, though by then it was nearly chore time.

Calico was amusing with the kittens. About two weeks

after they were born we felt they should live outside the house, as it was late spring, so we took them all in a box to a snug corner of the horse barn, where there was straw. Calico was not at all pleased with the arrangements and promptly hid her whole brood so well that we could not find them. One afternoon a month or so later she paraded out of the horse barn complacently with the whole crowd behind her. They were promptly named by the delighted children. There was a black-and-white one whose name I do not remember, one called Elizabeth, one called Buttercup, and an all-yellow male called Tommy.

The children enjoyed the whole tribe; indeed, we were all fond of them. They were just about full-grown when disaster struck. First the black-and-white one languished and died. Three days later, which happened to be the day before our first Christmas on the farm, Elizabeth and Buttercup died. Tommy disappeared, presumed dead somewhere.

We were much upset and took the cats for autopsy, learning an ancient lesson from the findings: all had died of strychnine. In the late autumn we had been particularly harassed by mice and rats in the cellar. On advice we sprinkled poisoned grain in cellar crannies. Apparently some poisoned mice went outside to die. The kittens may have found some themselves. Ironically Calico, who had been a most solicitous mother, selflessly fetching food for her brood long after their weaning, undoubtedly gave some of the deadly mice to them, for she herself survived the hecatomb. We have never used any poison since, in a household with pets.

Our misfortunes were not exclusively feline. The farm was an ideal place for a big dog. We had acquired our German shepherd from a good kennel and named him Ethan Allen.

We wanted him to be a proper working dog—to help us with the cattle, as indeed he did; do his traditional job of protecting Virginia's small flock of sheep; keep the abundant foxes away from the chickens and ducks; and further earn his keep as playmate and guardian of the children. He matured into a handsome dog and we were devoted to him.

The sheep were a quartet of Hampshire Downs of registered breeding; we had made an expedition with a hired truck in the first summer, across the ferry to a place near Ticonderoga, to acquire them. Their home, of course, was in the sheep barn, which could have housed a hundred. The small, choice meadow beside it, running from the lawn of the brick house down to the old milk house and the cattle barnyard, was fenced with sheep wire to contain them.

Early in March of our second year, Ethan went berserk one day and ran one of the sheep, harrying and biting it. I captured the dog and flogged him severely. The ways of German shepherds are unpredictable, both with people and animals. Occasionally, for no discernible reason, they become the destroyers of what they are supposed to guard. Virginia was immensely wrought up and demanded that the dog be killed. The children were thrown into wails at this thought. There was a good bit of friction all around.

I demanded probation for the dog, conceding that if it happened again he would have to go. To chain him up or pen him would only make him vicious. We confined him to a leash for quite a while, admonished him sharply whenever he was near the sheep, and after he was given free run again, tried to keep him in our company as much as possible.

In early April, only a little more than a month later, I heard distant shouts and screams. Rushing out of my office, I saw that some crisis had occurred down in the corner of the sheep meadow nearest the blockhouse. I ran as fast as I could. Virginia was trailing behind me. The sheep were huddled in the corner. Ann had climbed over the fence. She was sitting on the ground, her back braced against the fence, holding Ethan by the collar with both hands, digging her heels into the ground and straining to hold him. He was literally ravening—snarling and struggling, blindly bent upon a kill.

Scaling the fence, I took over the dog. Virginia drove her sheep back to the barn and shut them in, herself agitated to near hysteria, for which I couldn't blame her. Ann was pale, shaken, and exhausted. I got the dog under control and into the house, then within an hour drove him off to Dr. Miller's place and left him there to be disposed of—killed if necessary. Dr. Miller, who liked the dog, hoped to find him a home where there would be no animal temptations. I wouldn't have bet on the prospects. For the greater comfort of the children, who were much grieved at the loss, we never inquired.

A few hours later I found myself in pain and severely lame. Somehow, in the struggle with Ethan or the hasty fence hopping, I had torn ligaments in my foot. It swelled rapidly. The doctor in the village injected novocaine and bound it, and I hobbled about for a week or so.

Months later we acquired a puppy, a somewhat nondescript but amiable female, predominantly collie. Most succinctly described simply as a brown dog, she was named Brownie, and she greatly consoled the hearts of the children. A diligent harrier of woodchucks and helpful with the cattle, she was with us as long as we had the farm.

Sometimes our life in the blockhouse was a literal rat race. If you have led a sheltered enough life to have had no truck with these creatures you are fortunate. They are formidable and not pleasant to confront face to face.

Calico, who did a thorough job on mice, even got an occasional rat, which she always brought to show us proudly, aware that it was a feat of note. We always heaped glory, laud, and honor upon her at those times. I trapped a few also, but that was all that the rest of the cunning tribe needed to learn the idea, so the setting of the traps became a waste of time. In times before, we had made rat sandwiches with a hideous thick phosphorus paste that gave off a visible smoky fume and a loathsome smell. We spread it on bread with butter and sugar. Rats find these canapés irresistible; I think they eat them in the full knowledge that they will die of it. But after the disaster with the cats we were through with poisons altogether.

Later, when we occupied the brick house, we were free of the wearisome rodent war. The blockhouse was as vulnerable to them as to the probing winds. Strategically it was in a bad spot, flanked by cattle barn, horse barn, and piggery, all of which were good rat hide-outs. From these points they rallied to the warmth and lush attractions of a house with human occupants.

Oft in the stilly night, and at times even by daylight, we could hear them crunching—sapping and mining in their endless labors to shape the house to their will and convenience. This is demoralizing. The interior of the blockhouse had been finished with wallboard, which had been used for ceilings as well. Rats went through this like a wet paper bag. They chewed it for artistic effect as much as for access.

It was essential to keep all foodstuffs in metal containers. The rats investigated everything. It was a common experience for us to enter the kitchen, chiefly but not solely at night, and to have a rat casually jump down from a shelf or cupboard and dart behind the stove or refrigerator.

Of least practical annoyance but uncommonly vexing was the appearance of a neat round hole in the center of the kitchen ceiling. It was sheer insolence, as no rat wished, or needed, to plummet from ceiling to floor. It was simply a viewing post. Often, hearing a faint rustle, we would look up and see a rat, with his head thrust through, observing activities in the kitchen and filing away data for future reference.

One night Ann and I were reading aloud in our bedroom, both of us in robes and slippers, ready for bed. I went into the kitchen, which was opposite our bedroom door. A large rat jumped down from the shelves, came down facing me, and to my surprise, hesitated for a moment. I grabbed a broom, but before I could swing it the rat darted past me and into our bedroom, vanishing under the beds. Ann gave a yelp and leaped up at once.

We were both outraged, and I was angrily determined to get that rat. I hurried into the bedroom and shut the door. We felt we had him trapped—or he us—and that one side or the other would not leave that room alive.

Kneeling down cautiously, broom in hand, I looked under the beds. The rat was near the corner, crouched against the baseboard, returning my stare with reciprocal sentiment. I had nothing with which I could reach him. Then my eye fell upon an object near the door. It was a heavy iron doorstop, sufficient to finish him if I could clobber him with it. I grasped it firmly and knelt by the bed again. The rat was about ten feet away, fortunately in the lateral line of the wide, uneven floor boards. I bowled the weight at him with all my power and a sharpshooter's aim. The effort was naïve; the rat went up in the air and a little way forward. The doorstop splintered the baseboard and caromed off it futilely.

Retrieving the weight with the broom, I realized that a bowling or curling delivery was hopeless. Perhaps an aerial drop was possible. Ann, behind me, was holding a poker in self-defense. Gingerly I pulled the beds out from the wall by a foot or so. Now the rat was clearly exposed and in the light. He did not like this at all and darted his eyes about for a clear line of escape. Finding none, he stayed put in a temporary stand-off.

Then Ann thought of the kitten. Calico herself was out of the house, by bad luck, for she would have moved in unhesitatingly. But the children had another kitten upstairs, admitted as auxiliary house cat from among a later litter of Calico's. The kitten was inexperienced, but only a little less than full-grown. Could it cope? We decided to see.

Ann went and fetched the kitten. Shutting the door again, we dropped the little cat at the baseboard and watched. Each creature saw the other instantly. The cat bristled and was enthralled. Hesitantly it inched forward in the flattened feline stalking pose. The rat was motionless. The kitten advanced, paused, advanced. It came almost nose to nose; only inches separated them. That was that. The rat would not move but it was ready. The kitten knew that one more move would be an irrevocable commitment that it might regret making. They were what is now called eyeball to eyeball, waiting for a blink. This hypnotic tableau was held for a least five minutes.

Recognizing the impasse, I decided to try to take advantage of it to bomb the rat from the air. Cautiously I stepped up onto a bed, doorstop in right hand, broom still in left. My throwing motion caused the cat to glance up and the rat to bolt. The weight crashed again, squarely on target, with the rat no longer there. The kitten plunged under the bed in panic.

The instant the bomb had left my hand I was reacting to the rat's break-away. Feeling nakedly vulnerable in pajamas and loose slippers, I leaped off the bed swinging the broom. As the rat rounded the corner I came down hard with the flat of the broom on top of him. Good marksmanship, but it was no use. The weapon was too yielding, and the flattening capacity of rats and mice is extraordinary. As I raised the broom again the rat continued traveling, and in the same movement I saw our one miscalculation. I had forgotten the fireplace.

The rat began to claw its way up the rough brick surface of the interior wall. I took a mighty home-run swing and landed again with the broom. The rat fell down but it was unhurt, and before I could try again it made a successful leaping scramble and disappeared up into the flue.

A complete nervous wreck by this time, I got down with some disquiet and gingerly peered up the flue. The rat was there, staring down malevolently from the edge of the smoke shelf. The game was up. The thought of lighting a fire occurred to us, but there were easy access points from that old, complex masonry to space behind the wainscoting. To mix the metaphor, I had struck out but he was home safe.

The children, waked by all the crashing and banging, came down to see what was up and listened big-eyed to the tale. Graham and David thought it funny. Ann and I, like Queen Victoria, were not amused. The kitten was fetched from under the bed and taken back upstairs by the children. The beds were put back against the wall. But repose was poor that night, with the haunting image of something less benign than Santa Claus coming down the chimney.

CHAPTER EIGHTEEN

Book and Baby

THREE WINTERS in the blockhouse had brought us to the end of endurance. I felt that a fourth one would be the death of Ann, if not of the rest of us as well. The effort had been valiant and sometimes funny, but always with grim undertones.

There was an irony about the second and third winters. Virginia, who found she could not count on much winter business beyond an occasional literary client of mine, accepted a job as nurse-companion that took her to New York and Florida. The brick house was closed from early December until mid-April while we shivered and rattled down the hill. The idea of our moving up temporarily didn't seem feasible at the time, with all her things there and ours at the other house. We were still caught in the psychological compulsion of the harder way. So we held the line as it was, including taking over custody of Virginia's Scotch terrier,

Jeanie, who contributed a litter of wrong-side-of-the-blanket puppies to the second winter's divertissements.

Some new factors of many kinds were developing, however. During the first year Ann had undergone serious surgery in relation to an unsuccessful pregnancy. This had heightened our wish for a fourth child. Specialists in Burlington saw no reason why it should not be possible, even though Ann had other but less serious mishaps in the ensuing year and a half, once when we were down in Marlboro, Vermont, where I was co-director with John Farrar of a summer Fiction Writers' Conference at Marlboro College.

Early in 1951 the doctor confirmed that Ann had a good start on a pregnancy for which all conditions seemed promising. We felt we could make it through the rest of that winter but knew beyond question that things had to be changed. It was unthinkable to bring a new baby into the blockhouse for the next winter. Neither the space nor the living conditions nor the hard labor involved were tolerable in the new circumstances. After long negotiations we bought out Virginia's share in the farm. At the end of June we moved up to the brick house, the boys and I doing the work ourselves over several days with some hired help.

Compared to the blockhouse, life in the brick house even under summer conditions—let alone those of winter—was like a release from Purgatory. The ultimate comment on the blockhouse was a shock to us—a belated revelation. We had talked hopefully of renting it, and tried to do so. There were no takers. Then, when we speculated on the possibility of hiring a full-time man to operate the farm, it proved to be the stumbling-block house when we had tentative discussions with some farmers whose wives took one look and stalked away. We couldn't even pay anybody to live in it.

The brick house was warm, comfortable, and spacious. In addition to its living room we fitted up a library and music room. Everybody had a proper bedroom. For the first time since we came to the farm we could entertain with some grace.

It was well that we were in the brick house at last, for winter had reserved something special which caught us unexpectedly. I find it most compactly described in a February letter to Graham, who by then was away at school—of which more later.

Well, in the afternoon [of a Sunday] it started to snow, and by night it was a howling blizzard. Meanwhile, Meredith abruptly came down with a temperature of 103½, and we discovered we had no aspirin in the house, for once in our lifetimes.

In the morning the storm was still going on. It turned out to be the biggest thing we've seen since the great twenty-six inch fall in Nyack. This was almost, if not quite, as much fall, but had the element the other storm had lacked—high winds. Even as the snow slacked off in the morning, the winds howled on until night, increasing the drifts.

Of course we were isolated. It was the first time since we've lived here that we couldn't put on chains, and get out by hook or crook. Meredith was running high fever and we had to have aspirin. So David and I set out (I with a parka on) in the high winds and drifts, to get to L——'s [our immediate neighbors, who had taken over Paul's farm]. Talk about Scott of the Antarctic! The road to the mailbox, especially in the dip after you go around the corner from the driveway, was drifted full. It was up to my chest and almost impossible to break through. Poor Brownie became hopelessly lost in drifts and David and I had to fish her out a couple of times. [A neighbor's collie died in drifts.] Sometimes David and Brownie could walk on top of drifts but I never could.

The wind was ferocious. We made it, got the aspirin, and made it home. I seriously wondered if I could. Was totally exhausted and could well understand how it is possible just to drop and die under some circumstances.

We were plowed out Tuesday morning, only because I called and reported Meredith sick. We'd have been here 'til Wednesday otherwise, I guess. Some people were. Elithorpe said it was about the worst in his fifteen years as road commissioner. The plowed banks going out our road are higher than the car in places. One-car width and chains necessary.

Meantime, Meredith is getting well, but she had a severe bout with what I guess was a flu of some kind.

We encountered no other problems in the brick house except a vexing plague of flies that beset us just before the end of that first winter of comfort. They appeared principally in one second-story bedroom but spread elsewhere in the house from there. It was some time in March that they began to cluster as densely as a swarm of bees in the window frames. We could swat away at a thick carpet of them and shovel up the bodies in a dustpan. They were fat and black, somnolent and sluggish, and buzzed loudly and irksomely. Harley Cook called them sugar flies.

Swatting was futile. We laid in a massive munitions dump of bug bombs. Ann was investigating the mystery of the source of the invasion. They seemed to squeeze through minute spaces around baseboards or radiator pipes, from within the walls. We launched an all-out DDT attack in the bedroom. By the hundreds they dropped to the floor and spun dizzyingly round and round on their backs like buzzing midget pinwheels.

Ann suggested we go up to the attic. There we found the clue. They must have come in during the time the house was being remodeled, and formed an egg hatchery in the space between the inner and outer walls. By crawling into the eaves we could direct the bomb spray directly down into that space. Thousands of flies set up a hideous din, but we sprayed lavishly into the concentrated nests and elsewhere throughout the attic. That ended the plague.

Enormous changes had developed in the farm pattern and in the increasingly crucial balance between my life as a conspicuously inept farmer and my other life as a reasonably competent literary man. On the farm side, we had four head milking now, at an adequate production level: Susan, who had just graduated from heifer to cow, Daisy, Taffy, and Susan's second calf, Juniper. We had bought a second-hand milking machine, cooler, and other dairy equipment. I delivered a full can daily to the milk plant, fairly good for its nearly five percent butterfat content, and received modest checks every two weeks. They pleased me as symbols but were peanuts for the labor and investment involved. Milk never approached hay as an income source from the farm.

My professional work load was increasing and diversifying. I had many consulting clients, some obscure, some celebrated. This business was all by reference from agents and publishers, and later through the Writers' Conference. Sometimes I was working for the publisher, sometimes for the individual. The bulk of the work was a correspondence so voluminous that I had to buy a tape recorder and dictate bales of letters, which the town clerk would type for me as I shuttled the machine back and forth between us. A good many clients came to the farm, staying sometimes for a week or more at the brick house when Virginia was there, or in Middlebury otherwise. Occasionally I went down to New York, as I did for conferences when John Farrar called me in as an editorial aide for the memoirs of Judge Joseph M. Proskauer. The editing of the letters, papers, and journals of the late Leo Stein, Gertrude's brother, took me to New York and also to New Haven, to the Stein papers at the Yale Library. I wrote a critical study of George Bernard Shaw for Scribner's Twentieth Century Library series. Ever since arriving at the farm I had been working on my second novel. Then there was an active book-review schedule.

For two summers I was involved in the Marlboro Fiction Writers' Conference, which took up a good deal more time than the actual two weeks of its August sessions at the beautiful mountain-top campus of the small college not far from Brattleboro. The forgatherings there, in crises and comedy, would make a book in themselves, which if ever written, as Margaret Farrar once remarked pensively, should be called "The Lack of Foresight Saga." But it brought together fleetingly a fantastic congeries of personalities that included Bentz Plagemann, Charles Jackson, Vincent Sheean, Dorothy Thompson, Shirley Jackson, Stanley Hyman, Ludwig Lewisohn, Dorothy Canfield Fisher, Budd Schulberg, Merle Miller, and a great many others.

We had the boys with us at Marlboro part of the time each summer and Graham was old enough to enjoy himself thoroughly. David liked the mountains and the people but thought the endless round of lectures, classes, and bull-sessions a bore. Mavis McIntosh, the literary agent, who was both a friend and a colleague, was standing outside the main lecture hall on a starry night, taking a breather from the discourse within. She was under a spreading maple and became aware of a quiet chant going on somewhere above her head. A voice was repeating in a kind of litany, "I hate lecturers. I hate lectures. I hate lecturers. I hate lectures." She peered up through the leaves and discovered David Fuller, who had taken to the trees to ease his soul, as was his wont.

I spoke several times at Middlebury College, giving a number of Chapel addresses, taking part in one of their Annual Middlebury Conferences, on a three-day panel sequence with such diversely interesting men as Francis B. Sayre, Ira Wolfert, Foster Rhea Dulles, and William L. Shirer. Tangential to the college, President Stratton drafted me to deliver the town's annual Forefathers' Day address at the Congregational Church, preceding a dinner.

The operation of the farm was complicated further by my starting to make a few lecture trips under professional management.

An unexpected happening of major importance to us occurred just at the start of our second winter in the blockhouse, in 1949. I received a letter from the Vermont Commissioner of Education, Dr. A. John Holden, Jr., of Montpelier, asking me to meet him for lunch in Burlington. I couldn't image what that portended, but Ann and I went up to see.

Holden invited me to write an official history of the State of Vermont, to be used as a textbook in the public schools. The legislature had passed an act instructing the State Board to commission such a book.

I was astounded. "You don't want me!" I said. "I'm an outlander. By all tradition you should want a native Vermonter."

"I don't care about that," he replied. "We think you could do the job. Several people have spoken highly of you."

The original mover in the matter proved to have been John Hooper, editor of the *Brattleboro Reformer*, chairman of the State Board of Education, and also a trustee of Marlboro College.

Holden and I talked it over at length. I surprised him by stipulating that I wanted an official advisory board of distinguished scholars of Vermont history, whose names were to be on the title page of the book, and whose unanimous approval must be obtained before we published. It sounded to him like an encumbrance but I persuaded him that it was insurance. Nobody, let alone an outsider, could publish such a book without encountering some carping and objection. If we ran a stiff gamut first, we would be in a strong position to meet any later criticism. The point impressed him; he agreed, and we parted with a tentative commitment, mutually confirmed within a few days.

Ann and I drove home jubilantly. I was excited. I felt honored, challenged, financially relieved by the terms of the offer, and almost superstitiously amazed that such a bid had come to me who lived on one of the state's outstanding historic sites. It seemed as if it had been fated from that very January day when we waded through snow to discover Hand's Cove and were swayed in our purchase by the aura of its past.

The work on the history project extended from the end of 1949 until just before our departure from the farm in the summer of 1952. The finished product was in hand not long before we left. Writing the book had not been the end of it. Since there was no one else to do the job, I had to procure the illustrations and supervise every step of the physical manufacture of the volume as well.

It was a demanding, rich experience that carried me over the length and breadth of the state, into libraries and archives, bringing me into consultation with politicians, teachers, historians, writers, map makers, and specialists in a host of fields. Winter and summer, I rolled up thousands of miles of driving throughout the state. The help and support received from advisers, official and unofficial, defies cataloguing. The completed work was received generously and praised in many quarters, from the Governor down. The labor also generated a lasting friendship with John Holden, an able, and as the British say, "unflappable," administrator and devoted public servant, whose family roots ran deep and long in the state. His support and fellowship graced the whole adventure for me.

All during the Vermont years we had various problems about education. The school in the village was not good. There was only one principal of any quality while we were there and he shook off the limitations of the town for better fields before long. We were fortunate that for all the general mediocrity, both Graham and David each had one teacher who made a worth-while contribution to them. In each case it was an older married woman with the natural inborn grace of the true teacher, and an ability to strike a responsive chord in a lively young mind. They were much the best teachers and inspired long-lasting affection in the boys, who kept in touch with them for some time afterward. Yet both women were regarded as old-fashioned by their superintendent. They had to take education courses at one of the state teachers' colleges to keep their standing beside younger teachers who couldn't hold a candle to them.

We were not there long enough for the grade school problem to be serious, considering the stimuli and opportunities our children had at home. In the last year Meredith finally achieved her ambition to accompany the boys to school, but went only through first grade there.

When Graham entered the eighth grade—fortunately with his best teacher—we knew a problem lay ahead. The local three-teacher high school, in the same building, was so bad that the state office of education was trying hard to induce the village to abandon it and centralize—which the village stubbornly refused to do. It was out of the question for Graham's secondary education. We would have to send him away to school.

We applied for entrance to four schools: St. Paul's, Exeter, Andover, and Kent. We made trips with him for interviews at each of them, which involved elaborate arrangements about our cattle. In the case of Kent, we did the chores early before starting and did them late after returning from the more than three-hundred mile round trip. Graham took a stiff battery of entrance examinations. His performance was an immense credit to him, coming out of a tiny rural school. He was accepted almost simultaneously by St. Paul's, Andover, and Kent. We were so overwhelmed that we wrote at once to cancel the deliberations at Exeter, where there is every likelihood he would have been accepted too.

The choice was painful, as all of us liked all of the schools. We narrowed it to Andover and Kent, but Graham refused to express a strong preference one way or the other. The pull was so hard each way that I wrote a pair of letters to each school, one accepting, one declining. Ann and Graham referred the final decision to me after our inconclusive talks, so I took all four letters and two stamped envelopes to Middlebury for the night mail train. I sat for nearly an hour in my car at the station, undecided. As I heard the train approaching I committed a letter irrevocably to each of the envelopes, got out and dropped in the box a letter of acceptance to Kent and one of thanks and regrets to Andover. I could not have imagined the ramifications that were to flow from that hard choice.

Early in September of 1951, on a Sunday, I drove Graham down to Connecticut to leave him at Kent School. Again I did the milking just before starting and just after getting back, leaving the rest of the chores to David, who had now inherited Graham's role on the farm.

Graham and I were both emotionally agitated—he, worried about the lonely plunge into a new world; I, dismayed at the thought of leaving him. To me, a close-family man, it seemed like losing or abandoning him. He was supposed to be there for lunch at one o'clock. We barely made it, running up to the center entrance of the dining hall just as grace was about to be said.

Father Patterson, the headmaster of the famous Episcopal school, who had impressed us so deeply as to swing that final difficult choice to Kent, said, "Hello, son," to Graham, and propelled him toward a table before we could enter upon agonized farewells.

I blurted out the breathless confusion that possessed me, saying, "Well . . . I don't know what I should do now," half expecting to be bidden to lunch. Father Patterson said brusquely, "Frankly, sir, you should go home."

I did.

Though I was hungry, I drove for miles before stopping for food. There was a weight like a flatiron on my chest at the wrench of separation from our first-born. It was just as well that my feelings had their innings on the drive. There was no time for them when I got home.

The baby was due on September 25. The twenty-fourth, a Monday, was the publication day of my novel, *Brothers Divided*. Such an event often is as suspenseful as any other birth. The book had had a long, rough gestation, with its own dangers of miscarriage.

My mother was at the farm already, and on the morning of the twenty-fourth my oldest sister and her husband stopped briefly. Ann and I departed for Burlington and went first to the doctor, who started Ann on quinine, to be continued through the afternoon. Then we visited Professor Leon Dean at the university, one of my official advisers on the history textbook, and then our friend Ralph Hill, among the unofficial ones.

We went next to the principal bookstore of Burlington and saw a large display of *Brothers Divided* in its window. I was interviewed there by a young woman from the *Free Press* and signed a batch of books. That was my show, but it was much the minor one of the unfolding moment.

Ann and I could have dined with Ralph or a choice of other pleasant friends but we chose to have dinner by ourselves, in the best restaurant we could find in Burlington. There was music, and we laughed, and hoped—for both book and baby—and we dissembled our anxiety—for both book and baby.

At seven-thirty Ann entered the Mary Fletcher Hospital and was promptly given a liberal dose of castor oil. I stayed with her as long as I was allowed, and when I was sent away to wait, the memories of the physical mischances of the last three years overwhelmed briefly in my mind the prior record of three fine births. I was as frightened as a novice father—or rather more so.

My diary entry for the twenty-fifth begins:

> Little girl born about 2:20. Janet Faith Fuller, to be called Faith, for she is an act of faith. Ann and baby both fine. Saw baby and talked a little with Ann when she came down. All went smoothly as with other babies born before the troubles. Got home at 5:00, dead tired, after driving slowly for sleepiness. Up at 7:00.

Janet, the unused part of Faith's name, was the name of the heroine of *Brothers Divided*. The next few days were turbulent. I went back and forth to Burlington daily, visiting Ann and Faith, signing more books in Burlington and also in the Middlebury store of our friend Dike Blair. Trips to the hospital were combined with ones to Montpelier for history conferences.

Obviously I couldn't be milking my little herd in the midst of this. Ed Douglas had taken over all the milking stock for me in his own barn. David took care of the dry cattle.

On the thirtieth, after we had set up once more our thrice-used rickety crib, my mother, David, and I went to Burlington to bring home Ann and Faith. It was a joyous mission. At Ann's wish, Faith was held by her admiring grandmother on the ride home.

Faith was delicately lovely from the start, the tiniest of our babies, a mere mite just about big enough to cradle in a match box, but beautifully modeled. The other children marveled at her smallness. The book that was launched into the world with her was as nothing and went its way as others before and after. Faith was the enduring reward of the Vermont years, the hardest gained and the most cherished.

My mother went home and our household ticked along smoothly. Early in October we had another surprise visit from Judge and Mrs. Augustus Hand, who duly admired Faith and were delighted at the Vermont history project being carried out on the old place.

Their visit prompted me to reflect upon and to identify ourselves with the closing words of the dedication Mrs. Hand had set at the head of the volume of family letters:

> They also reveal certain traits of character, which I trust, you and your descendants, will continue to possess; A sober view of life; A respect for Education, and a determination to obtain it; And an extraordinary family loyalty.

It was no wonder that the aura of the farm was good.

About two weeks later both David and Meredith were home from school with colds and fever. We watched them carefully but it was our ears, not our eyes, that gave us the frightening news; we had whooping cough in the house.

We called Ann's doctor in Burlington immediately and he referred us to the city's best pediatrician. What were we to do with this fragile infant? The whooping cough, a notorious infant killer, could carry her off in short order. We moved Meredith downstairs to David's room, as far from the baby as possible. I canceled a trip to Montpelier. We had to disappoint poor homesick Graham by calling off a promised weekend at home.

The doctors were uncertain what to do about Faith. She might or might not catch whooping cough; if she did, she might or might not die. The Burlington pediatrician knew of a new serum of human antibodies but had never used it. We had to decide.

We phoned an uncle of Ann's in Annapolis, Maryland, a distinguished public-health doctor. He was acquainted with the serum and endorsed it. Our Burlington man telephoned to Philadelphia for it to be sent by air.

Two days later we took Faith to Burlington in bitter cold. The pediatrician gave her a 10cc. injection of serum in the buttocks. It seemed a huge dose for such a small infant, and for all our efforts at composure we flinched at the stab. Faith squalled woefully but did not get the whooping cough. Our sole native Vermonter already was hardy.

The following weekend, tired but with a feeling of crisis past, I departed to visit Graham at Kent. It was Mothers' Weekend, but as Ann could not go and Graham was homesick, I went and put in the best performance I could muster as his mother. We fooled no one.

CHAPTER NINETEEN

Dear Hearts
and Gentle People

VERMONT GAVE US our first intensive experience of small-town life. One might be tempted to modify that by "American," or "New England," or some other qualifier or localizer, but my instinct is against modifiers. Markedly differing regional characteristics do exist but I am sure that the essence of the small town is universal, because it rests upon that greater universal—human nature.

People who live in cities are different only superficially from those in small towns, though the differences are real. There are single apartment houses in New York that hold more families than lived in our Vermont village. But while great cities reveal special facets of human nature in their streets, apartments, and offices and through what the press reports of them, they also mask a great deal that is laid bare in the rural town. There is an anonymity to cities and to vast apartment complexes that the small town does not know.

The town is the microcosm, the viewing screen, the laboratory specimen of much human behavior. This accounts for the perennial fascination and popularity of small-town-exposé fiction, from the finest to the shoddiest—let's be specific—from *Spoon River Anthology* and *Winesburg, Ohio* to *King's Row* and *Peyton Place*.

Is it true what they say about small towns? Whatever you want to put into the mix—it's all true; it's all there: adultery, incest, and seduction in their infinite varieties; murder, theft, fraud, blunder, brutality, stupidity, sloth, greed, insanity, hatred, bigotry—in short, the seven deadly sins and their seventy-times-seven corollaries.

It is also possible to find in small towns the cardinal virtues: honor and integrity, diligence, common sense and sometimes wisdom, compassion and simple kindness, faith, fidelity, and perseverance in adversity.

During our Vermont sojourn a triumphantly banal song became popular, saccharine in words and tune, about "dear hearts and gentle people" in small towns. It was seized upon with particular glee by Graham, who had achieved a precocious disenchantment with the romantic vision of small-town life.

If the people of our village, or of Vermont in general, were to think that I am gunning for them, it is not so—particularly. All one need do is change the name, be it of town, state, or country—the elemental human face is still familiar.

Once I passed through a place called Flat Rock, North Carolina. It seems to me that it would serve excellently as the generic name of all small towns in the world. Look beneath the surface and you will find in all of them everything that is associated with the undersides of flat rocks. But when the chips are down—or even when the rocks are up—I would rather live in any of the Flat Rocks, or Vermont towns—you name them—than in the steel-and-concrete hives of urban renewal projects. Humans aren't much at the best but they won't improve if you deliberately dehumanize them by compressing them in cubicles.

Many people in the village were very kind to us and warmly friendly. I am speaking of those who helped us with practical problems without being involved in any sort of cash transaction touching the working of our farm—who had no profit to make from us.

There were many times when I found myself in a real jam with our few cattle, especially when we reached the point of milking four cows by machine and selling milk at the creamery. Ed Douglas often came to my help, advising me, showing me, or pitching in directly with me to do a job. Ed easily might have had contempt for me, as some surely did, because I was not a master of his skills. But he knew there were skills of which I *was* master, and in his own sphere he was generous and kind.

One Sunday afternoon in November the boys and I spent several hours at the Douglases', at the pleasant task of making cider with his hand press. We turned a big wheel to exert the pressure on the chopped, mashed apples, and the machine reminded me a little of an early hand printing press. Some juicy things, sweet or hard, were pressed out in ink by Gutenberg and his heirs.

I mentioned to Ed that I was having a rough time with Taffy, who had mastitis. The illness plugged her teats, which had to be squeezed out, and she kicked from pain almost more than I could control.

Next morning at six o'clock I had just started chores in my barn when I heard a car come down the hill. It was Ed, who had come unasked to help me with Taffy, and who worked through my whole routine with me to get things in better shape. When the demands of my professional work forced me out of dairying permanently, Ed took over all my milkers on a rental basis and supplied us with milk also, which we picked up each evening at his barn.

Bill Stalker, the young neighboring orchardist, and his wife, Nancy, welcomed us. They knew something of a world outside the village beyond the borders of Vermont; they were often a comfort as well as a practical help to us and I believe our presence was a pleasure to them. One season, for the sake of the experience, I donned a picker's apron in the apple-picking time and put in a few days' work in Bill's orchard with other townspeople and the transient migratory pickers.

Russell Easton, truly a gentle person, brought the mail on the rural delivery route. From the beginning he was fascinated by the volume of mail and books that I received. When there was a lot he would bring it all the way in, rather than put it in the mailbox on the outer road, which was all duty required. We shared a cup of coffee and talked and philosophized often. His wife, Florence, was organist in the Congregational Church, and often I practiced with her for solos I rashly sang as a sometime choir member.

Among our best friends were Harley Cook and his wife, Esmé. They were much older than we; Harley was in his seventies and died at about the time we left. He was the truest archetypal Vermonter I ever knew; tall, lanky, deliberate in speech and movement, white-haired and lean of face, matter-of-fact and terse in comment, capable of a penetratingly wry, utterly dead-pan humor. He was a carpenter but also knew just about every phase of farming.

Esmé was a warm-hearted, plump country housewife without a streak of malice in her. She could extend herself in affection to many people. Deeply religious in a kind of fundamentalist piety, she was not a bigot and could give help to people in duress whose behavior she could neither understand nor approve in her own moral code. She had charity. There were far more sophisticated and complicated people in the town, calculated to shock her deeply, to whom Esmé gave her warm hand in time of trouble, without stint or judgment.

We grew increasingly fond of Harley and Esmé in the course of our years there and often called for his advice. Hesitantly he undertook to build for us, from a design we showed him in a book, a Colonial-style pine sideboard with shelves and scroll trimming. He was not a cabinetmaker, he insisted, and said throughout the job, "Well, we don't know what it's going to be until we get through with it."

It worked out well and we still have it in our dining room, an honest piece of plain craftsmanship. Harley's accounting of costs on it were meticulous to the last nail, and the greatest fee that I could persuade him to take was modest.

And yet—we had no intimate companionship with true kindred spirits within close range of us. We had to go many miles for the few friends who spoke our language fully. We were not inherently better than our neighbors and local friends, but we were inherently different from them. We were artists, creative people, definitely committed to a vision of life that reached beyond the horizons, interests, and awarenesses of a conventional rural community. There were questions always in our minds which never presented themselves to our neighbors, inquiries which they were not called to pursue, and enterprises which they did not share.

In the old game of "What's wrong with this picture?" it was *us*. Our local friends valued us in varying degrees for ourselves and were intrigued by us as exotics. The others held us in undisguised mild contempt and suspicion, or counted us mere objects of curiosity.

Curiosity was a constant, all right. Small towns are powered by it in large measure. People listened in on the party line—there were twelve parties on ours, including a sawmill. The hand-cranked phones have gone. With the dial system there is no longer an omniscient local operator to say, "She ain't home now, but you can get her over to Johnsons' "—such information sometimes flung into the middle of a conversation you had not realized was being monitored. In the village certain women sat all day at the window—what they didn't know they guessed, what they couldn't guess they made up. Every time we passed through in our car we knew we were being checked by someone for who was with us, how we were dressed, and how soon we would come back again.

The general store vied with the post office and the corner filling station as the center of gossip. Old-timers sat by the hour saying "Yep!" "Yessirree!" and "Ayeh!" about fishing, crops, weather, and their neighbors' personal conduct. An aged hired man on old-age pension, with no family, sat all day every day in the store, toothless, gumming his tobacco, and cackling with gossip and reminiscence. He loved liquor so much and got so little that he was reputed to drink up all the hair tonic, toilet water, and mouth wash in the house where he boarded.

The supposed rural paradise for our children was an illusion also—264 acres of lovely land was not enough. They needed education and the companionship of children whose future patterns of life could be expected to have something in common with theirs. These things were absolutely lacking.

Our position was awkward. Any criticism we made, any improvement we sought was resisted because we were outsiders, aliens, accused of thinking ourselves and our children to be better than other people. What was good enough for the entrenched townfolk was not good enough for us.

The school system was one of the principal instruments through which the village in effect drove out many newcomers who might have lifted the level of the community. This went on all the years we were there, we learned of instances before our time, and we know of cases since. The location and possibilities of the village attracted to it various persons of intellect, and sometimes of wealth also. Within a few years most of them gave up and left, at which part of the town chortled with triumphant glee, sinking back into its complacent littleness. Others mourned.

Our children had many acquaintances in the town, some of them nice children of character and worth; but there were no common paths ahead, no discernible permanencies of relationship, no similar goals or expectations.

Ann and I found that for the kind of exchange we needed urgently, we had to drive at least the twenty-one miles to Middlebury, where in the context of a college town we found friends of our own kind, not all of whom were college people. Our best friends in Vermont—like ourselves now long gone from there—lived a good forty miles away, but the drive was worth it: Clement and Edith Hurd, he a painter and she a writer of children's books. Chad and Eva Walsh, who came with their daughters to spend summers in Vermont, were devoted friends. Thus, from Middlebury, to Charlotte (pronounced in Vermont with a strong accent on the second syllable), to Burlington, even indeed to Montpelier, and also down in the southern and eastern sections of the state, we had a network of friendships, but the pursuit of them was arduous across this spread of geography and with the hazards of winter.

By and large it seemed to us that the Yankee farmer was withering on the vine. There were, and are still, Vermont farmers of Anglo-Saxon stock, but they are losing ground. Apart from the relatively small amount of good tillable land in the state, several other factors tell against them.

There was a vast shove westward from New England in the nineteenth century. Stewart H. Holbrook has chronicled this excellently in *The Yankee Exodus*. The remaining stock shows a slow diminishing of vitality. It is hard and expensive to get adequate help. The children tend to leave the farm, and often the state as well.

For a long time the French Canadian has been moving onto ground vacated by the Yankee. One of the things that draw him to and sometimes make him a problem in Vermont is the fact that bad as anything there may be, starting with the quality of a piece of land, it is generally better than what he was able to have in Canada, so for him it is a gain, it is opportunity.

Generalizations about the French Canadian in Vermont are dangerous, especially if based upon the French-speaking new immigrant. One or two generations in Vermont make a vast difference. Gregoire, the best plumber in town, with the appearance of a classical Yankee, was manifestly of French origin. Allen Mayville of the U.S. Soil Conservation office and Lucien Pacquette, the county agent of the State Farm Bureau, were of French roots, both college-trained men serving the public for the betterment of the land.

Often you would find a home with the grandparents speaking only French, the next generation speaking badly broken

English, but their daughters going to the state teachers' college to supply the need of the schools. Balanced against this long-range contribution is the fact that in the annual March Town Meeting, the French farmers tended to vote solidly against measures much needed to improve the schools. The incentive to education was not high, and by their standards and past experience the schools were quite as good as they saw any need to have them be. They weren't eager to be taxed to make them better.

March Meeting is a quintessential Vermont town experience—exhilarating and exasperating by turns. It is a primal unit of basic democracy, thrashing out the budget for everything from schools and roads to bombing woodchuck holes and cutting grass in the cemetery. Every facet of human nature is exhibited there, from avarice to zeal for the public good. Luke Buttolph, who had long been the Moderator in our village, had the flavor and tone of the Stage Manager, the narrator in Thornton Wilder's *Our Town.*

The small-town Congregational churches were not in a vigorous state. Attendance was rather thin. But outside the Roman Catholic churches, including ones where the priest came from another town for a single Mass on Sunday, the cars and trucks of the French farmers lined up. For them it was essentially the authoritarian peasant church of Quebec Province, and sometimes in these rural Vermont Roman churches the sermons were preached in French. Yet here, as was often true on the farms, was the sign of something robust in contrast to something wilting.

On the farms the great French resource, the competitive edge against the Yankee was sons. It was not uncommon to find six or more sturdy sons out of a family that might run to fourteen children. The Yankee farmer had far fewer sons, of whom still fewer stayed to work the farm for long. The French families were organized on the peasant tradition: Grand-père was the patriarch, Papa the tyrant, the sons the obedient subjects. Grand'mère and Maman, commonly speaking only French, were honored in their domestic roles but it was a male-dominated world.

To the formidable in-group manpower of these families were added spreading networks of brotherly, cousinly, or merely fellow-French solidarity, to be tapped in mutual labor aid for emergencies or special seasonal work thrusts. Sometimes—not always—they were crude, wasteful, primitive, backward, even destructive farmers, yet they could get by, or wax prosperous by their standards, on sheer gross, muscular energy.

The Yankee farmer, often a loner dependent upon transient hired help and the co-operation of friends, would sometimes be a progressive farmer, not by native virtue but by a combination of necessity and education. He had to be efficient to survive, had to use the best methods he knew, and the best machinery and equipment he could procure. For breeding his cows he was likely to use the Artificial Breeders Association; the French-Canadian farmer was likelier to keep a sullen scrub of a bull.

Many new immigrants, and, for that matter, some old Yankees, were contemptuously disdainful of all modern methods and of those who practiced or endorsed them. To see this psychology in operation, read *Anna Karenina* and note the stubborn resistance of the peasants to the agricultural innovations introduced by the progressive Konstantin Levin.

Occasionally among the old Vermont stock we would see hostility toward the French Canadian. It was always a matter of private expression when they were with their own, but what anthropologists call the we-group, they-group attitude was definitely there and was mutual. We always need somebody to view with distaste, suspicion, or anxiety. It must be a minority, but one big enough to be felt significantly as a constant presence and also as a threat; an economic rival, a usurper and producer of social change.

Our direct experience with French farmers involved one instance that conformed to the above generalizations, and one that was an exception to them.

A neighboring farmer who had gotten out the horses and sled on the snowy January day when we first saw Hand's Cove was a Frenchman who had been there a long time and who worked his farm well. A rare exception to the large-family pattern, he had only one son. We had liked this farmer, who spoke an accented English, but with a certain dignity and grace. "Your farm is very beautiful and peaceful under the snow," he troubled to add to a neatly written letter, in answer to some questions not long after we had bought the property.

When we moved in, he informed us that he was retiring and had just sold his farm to his son, who was taking over at once. This was a disappointment to us. The son was strong and certainly knew how to farm, if he could keep his mind to it. He may have hoped to exploit us and was quick to make sharing arrangements, and was indeed quite affable and helpful in a rough way. But he was casual and erratic in performance and had to be pressed to make cash settlements. He would agree to do things in approved ways as the experts had advised us, but with obvious scorn and the intention to ignore these practices if not watched closely.

Something of a wild boy, he grew increasingly restless.

There were troubles between himself and his young, frail, battered, anemic-looking wife. We had decided that we wanted to be shut of him well before he chucked the whole business abruptly and took off. His farm was taken over by a quiet, hardworking relative, with whom we had no transactions but lived in courteous neighborliness.

A year or so later our other, steadier farmer—non-French—decided that he no longer stood in need of the sharing arrangements with us. This left us in a jam.

A large French family, the Marceaus, had recently moved onto a farm down the road just within the limits of practical proximity. I approached them, or they me—I don't remember. They were new, ambitious, and hungrily quick to make a deal.

The negotiations went on over several sessions, partly at our place and partly at theirs. On both sides almost the entire family listened in. Étienne Marceau, bulky and ham-handed, was the managing operator of the farm. He was not articulate, I suspected, even in his own patois. Grand-père—whom I came to address as such in time—was the patriarchal clan head and did the greater part of the talking. His English was much better than Étienne's. The old man was quite fragile, with shiny, parchment skin. He was a natural if primitive gentleman. He still worked a little, but at light skills. Étienne and the grandsons treated him with veneration.

The transactions were complicated, many-faceted, touching upon pasture rentals, hay sharing, division of baling expenses, plowing and reseeding of meadow for me, cutting of wood for me and assistance at times with fence work, and the spreading of my painfully small stock of manure.

Grand-père was courteously agreeable to all my stipulations about good practice, though Étienne and his sons were overt in their scorn of such frippery. Yet an open convenant was at last openly arrived at.

During these and all subsequent conversations with the Marceaus, Graham noticed in me a tendency to fall into a barbarous dialect that matched the Marceaus' speech, accompanied by much shrugging and arm-waving. He considered this deplorably phony and hypocritical on my part. But it was a natural process of communication across so immeasurable a gap in articulateness. Anyway, if not a shrugger, I am certainly something of an arm-waver, and the tendency to fall into a regional pidgin is one that I have since found comes to me in all non-English-speaking countries once I have run out of my limited language resources.

On the whole the Marceau deal worked satisfactorily. Mostly, except for the big push on haying, it would be one or more of the older sons who would come to do tasks on our place. The oldest said little but always laughed at whatever he saw done by any of us. Another one, in marked contrast, was a great talker, with total confidence, and would explain to us the folly of all our ways. He suffered from a hernia. It could happen to anyone, but was notably common among this class of the French who sometimes were as carelessly wasteful and destructive of human as of animal resources. One saw many youthful French farm workers severely and permanently damaged in bone and muscle. There were always others coming to fill the place.

The disquieting thing for us about the Marceaus was a sense that they were waiting to move in. It was a bit like sharing a farm with Genghis Khan. This subtle pressure of the rude doers lurking to take over from the effete dreamers was something that we all felt.

It was poor Graham who got the direct prod, unremittingly, in a primitive psychological warfare waged, of all places, on the school bus. One of the younger boys, Raoul, impatiently marking his brief time in the school, would plunk himself in the seat beside Graham and launch upon some variation on a constant theme: "You can't farm . . . Your father don't know nothin' about farmin' . . . You don't belong on that farm . . . Someday *we're* gonna have your farm!" Then he would extol the Marceau tribe and brag of his lusty brothers.

Graham found it oppressive. He wouldn't have known it as such, then, but it was his first encounter with the insecurity of the intellectual when thrust outside his field, competing at a disadvantage with rude mechanicals. Possibly it came back to him at moments in the Slavic studies in which he took his Harvard master's degree, as an anticipation of Khrushchev's "We will bury you."

CHAPTER TWENTY

A Reckoning

THE ENTERPRISE that began with a convulsion ended with a paralysis. The former was literal; the latter is a metaphor, but we had seen the handwriting on the barn wall.

Let me not blink the facts. The venture did fail. We knocked ourselves out—almost literally for Ann, for which I felt a deep repentance. What ever possessed me to imagine that I could operate a farm? Harley Cook, in the final year of our stay, expressed the fallacy crisply. He had watched me at work; he knew all phases of our operations over a long time. One day he remarked, quite kindly, "Edmund, your labor as a farmer is worth about twenty-five cents an hour. You'd be better off to write your books and let other people do the rest."

But how were we to dispose of this property? Where would we go and what would I do next? The farm was now harder to sell than when we had bought it. We had put a lot of money into it, but the catch was that this had gone into special kinds of improvements—not the kind that improved it as a farm. We could never recoup our stake by selling to a working farmer. It was now distinctly an estate; it must be sold to a city person, at the most a gentleman farmer, a person of means who could afford to pour far more into its further development than ever we could. We had to wait for a buyer in a narrowing field.

Also I had come too far away from my professional base, even as a free lance. When necessary, I had to be able to get in and out of New York with greater frequency, ease, and less expense. It was important that I no longer be anchored to something that I could not leave without elaborate arrangements that tied up other people.

In the kind of rural limbo to which we had awakened at last, I think it seemed to Ann that I was not facing reality, because I behaved as if we were going to continue. I knew as well as anyone that we had to get off the farm—and that right quickly—but my way of resisting despair was to be affirmative as long as we had to remain. I could not sit down in a corner of the barn and throw straw over my head, keening the while.

Then an offer came. The managing editor of a large publishing house asked me to come to New York for a talk with him. It was early spring of '52. I went down and was offered the chief editorship of the house at a starting salary larger than anything I had ever earned, with a schedule of bonuses and raises. The managing editor with whom I would work closely was a congenial person.

I said I would go back and confer with Ann and make a decision as quickly as I could. I seemed to have no option. It might be the providential answer to everything. I was grateful but at the same time reluctant. It was a demanding assignment that would tie me to a full-time desk regimen with the inescapable permeation of one's life that any such job entails —in short, it was a job demanding all energies, not measured by hours. At the very best I would have to live within commuting range and stay in town some nights. Possibly we would have to live right in the city.

I knew I had the abilities for this kind of career, and it had a dangerous lure for me—dangerous because it was not how I wanted to live. It was not the road which I really wanted to take. But in other words of Frost, I had promises to keep. Yet it seemed to me that I would fail to keep other promises if I accepted.

I got to Middlebury in the early morning after the sleepless Pullman ride. Ann met me and we drove back to the farm. I was tired, and happy insofar as I saw a way to end the game and could not indulge my reservations about it. Ann, too, felt deeply relieved.

We hadn't been home very long when the phone rang. The operator said that it was Father Patterson calling from Kent. This had never happened before. It smacked of emergency. I thought that Graham must be either dead or expelled, and it was with anxiety that I heard the headmaster's voice. With his customary directness he said, "Mr. Fuller, would you consider taking a position in our English department?"

I nearly dropped the phone. All I could say was, "I don't know. I've never thought of such a thing."

He said, "Will you think about it? Will you come down here and talk with us about it?"

In a few days I did so. It was characteristic of John Patterson to think that his English department might gain something from the presence of a professional literary man who had never been in the academic field. I knew that I liked to teach, but couldn't know how I would like teaching at the secondary level.

Financially the offer couldn't compare with the publishing one. Yet it meant a wholly different choice about life. We would not live in the city, nor would I commute. It was stipulated that I would have no coaching duties or any other such tasks customary in schools. I would do my teaching, contribute what I could to the development of the school's English curriculum, and otherwise be master of my time to do my other literary work. John Patterson wanted me to go on with writing and criticism. In effect I was to be writer-in-residence at a school.

I happened to see John Farrar, and though we had already made up our minds, out of curiosity I confided the alternatives to him and asked what he thought I should do. Without an instant of hesitation he said, "Go to Kent."

That was what we did. We have never regretted it. Just as the decision we had made about a school for Graham had developed this unanticipated ramification, still further ones lay ahead.

Meanwhile Professor Donald Clark, who was then head of English at Columbia University's School of General Studies, invited me to teach a course in creative writing at the summer session. We accepted that, in a progressive move that took us from Vermont to Columbia early in the summer and from Columbia to Kent at its close. The session at Columbia was followed by an invitation to teach their evening course in Comparative Literature through the ensuing academic year, which I did with pleasure but declined the further invitation to continue because the trips in and out by car from Kent were too taxing.

A *Reckoning*

So it was that we left the farm in the early summer of 1952, after four years. We disposed of all creatures and closed the place, putting it in the hands of agents. Our good angel continued with us: the place was sold by the next November, to city people, and we got out of it with no capital gain but only a modest loss.

Now for the totting up, the reckoning. In the title of Clare Kummer's old comedy, the move to the farm was "A Successful Calamity." It was a mistake, yet I think a gallant mistake, a growth-inducing mistake, an onward-leading mistake. If Providence indeed watches over sailors, drunken men, and fools, It had watched over us. We had accepted a challenge, but it had proved to be what Toynbee calls an over-challenge.

Hand's Cove was a lovely place, even if sometimes rigorous. The basic disillusionment of our romantic idyll was the brutal fact of my inability to cope with the farm. The other was that we found ourselves isolated from communion with our own kind. It was our own fault for trapping ourselves in these two circumstances—my fault especially. Both facts were foreseeable. We had lost sight for a while of who we were, and to that extent the Vermont adventure was a rediscovery of identity.

We tried to adapt, and tried our best to give something as well as get something. We flung ourselves into the community. Ann staged pageants for the church and spoke at PTA meetings. Together we were on panels on behalf of conservation and poured ourselves into the effort to make our farm a laboratory for it, but we lacked the means to carry it through. I served as a town library trustee and left many good books there. Chiefly, I left the history textbook behind me in the schools. Yet we found in time that we were overadapting strenuously and losing ourselves.

At the same time we *had* changed during the farm years, in tangible ways. We had set out in an attempt to find certain values for ourselves, and though the farm was not to be a permanent plantation, it served as the matrix in which we reappraised our lives. It was as if we had experienced an equivalent of the traditional "wilderness period," the withdrawal and return, in which men sometimes have sought to discover themselves.

Perhaps part of what happened can be expressed most briefly in the odd history of my novel, *Brothers Divided*. I had begun to plan it before we went to Vermont, and had signed a contract for it with my publisher. It was to be about a young minister of my generation who found the Christian faith untenable and withdrew from the vocation.

As a craftsman I knew that much research was needed. For this I went to Union Theological Seminary, in New York, and sought out its dean, David E. Roberts, who died most untimely some years later. He was my contemporary and had studied at Union in the years of the thirties, about which I was to write. With full knowledge of my intentions he gave me the run of the seminary. I visited classes, used the library, and ate in the dining halls. Roberts introduced me to Reinhold Niebuhr, who talked helpfully with me about the period.

My novel turned out to be not a rejection but an affirmation of faith. No one was as surprised as I, who had been reared as a Presbyterian but had fallen away from the Church. The interior developments that had drawn me to the subject in the first place were other than I had thought.

During the farm years these processes led us through a closer and closer examination of where we were bound and what we believed. The shocking crisis of Ann's near death under surgery was another element in our course. Before we left Vermont we had entered the Episcopal Church, in Middlebury, I by Confirmation—Ann had been brought up in it. Our children, too, were baptized there. Graham, at twelve, grumbled, "Why didn't you have us baptized when we were babies—this is so embarrassing." Only one answer was possible: "Because we didn't believe in God when you were babies—we do now."

This was the pivotal development of our lives in the farm years and there can be no doubt that the experience was inextricably related to it in ways I could not trace without great difficulty. The new commitment determined our choice of a school for Graham, and in its surprising aftermath helped sway my decision to go to Kent. Beyond this, it permeated my thought in ways that shaped my subsequent work as writer, critic, and teacher.

It is not intended to pursue those interior events and their outward signs in this book—yet not to mention them at all would be to leave a blank at the point where lies the meaning of the whole adventure and its consequences. The family that left the farm was different from the family that went there. In that difference lay the gain that more than counterbalanced the failure.

Of the adventures and activities on the farm, retained in the memories of the children and ourselves, and recorded in my diaries and letters, these chapters do not contain the tenth part, but they have captured essences.

If the agricultural accomplishments were negligible except for comic effect, the professional work fared remarkably well, all considered. George Britt had feared I would plunge into obscurity, but when I left the farm I was better known professionally back in New York than when I had set out. Three books had been written and published, and one compiled, in addition to reviews and articles, and there was work in progress.

David felt the deepest pang as we left, saying wistfully, "I love every pebble on this farm." For all of us there are impressions that cling. Remembrances visit my mind unexpectedly by day or night. They come especially with changing seasons, or the odor of mowed grass with its hint of hay, with high wind, or the color of the sky, or the sight of cattle, or the glint of light on a blue lake.

We are gone from there, the farm has been twice sold and once divided. I've been back a number of times, most recently at the concluding of this writing, which is May, 1965. The place is greatly changed and is altogether an estate. All the barns and outbuildings except a rebuilt garage are gone; the brick house is remodeled extensively (and expensively). The blockhouse, on the other hand, has been neglected. The work we did to make it livable has been partly pulled out—I don't know why—and the interior is a shambles.

Ann and I prowled through it by permission, our sophisticated Siamese cat poking in curiosity in the rubble where once Calico had patrolled. The house seemed small and bleak. On the white-painted drainpipe coming down from the bathroom, Ann spotted a curious surviving trace—a penciled telegraph message on the pipe, beside where the phone had been. It was from *Saturday Review*: "Will you review Neither Five Nor Three, by Helen McInnes. Need 500-600 wds. Feb. 28 deadline." It had come in on a cold day, that is sure.

Outside, a Chinese elm we had planted by the treeless blockhouse now reached as high as the chimney. The pond was full and clear, lined attractively by grassy banks and shrubs. It was strange to see the big barn and smaller buildings gone, but all was open and beautiful.

With my small dog, I walked in the sun down to the cove and the point—all fences gone. The cove was unchanged, the redwing blackbirds busy—I could have expected to see David beside me, and old Tommy hunkered down by his fishlines as on the day we met him, seventeen years before. That seemed far away.

But there was change. Along the north bank of the point was a substantial, dense, narrow grove of spruce and white pine from the great planting. I had to push my way through it at places. It was high above my head. I looked at the clay banks—they are still crumbling—those thousands of shrubs did not survive—mere patches left, the rest slipped away. The black locust failed, too. Yet the pine is there, vigorous, even ready to be thinned. The multiflora rose seems to have been rooted out deliberately on this section of the farm, with the extensive removal of fences. There were substantial patches of it along the woods on the north part of the farm, now still held by the one to whom we sold it. These plantings and the pond are our remaining traces on the landscape. One might say that *we* had got no good out of it. But we got the good of doing it, and there is no doubt some good was done.

From our base at Kent we have moved around a good deal since, living at times in Mexico and in England. As this is written, we are packing for an intended long residence in Rome, where I shall again write and teach English, at St. Stephen's School, which our former Kent headmaster and good friend, John Patterson, has established there with the kind of gallantry to which we vibrate in resonance. So, in the classic way, for us even the road to Vermont has turned out to be the road to Rome.

ABOUT THE AUTHOR

EDMUND FULLER has worked as author, editor, critic, and teacher. He has written three novels, *Brothers Divided*, *A Star Pointed North* and *The Corridor*, as well as diversified non-fiction, including *Man in Modern Fiction* and *Books with Men Behind Them*. His reviews and articles have appeared in the *New York Times*, the *Herald Tribune*, *Saturday Review*, the *Chicago Tribune*, the *Wall Street Journal*, and *American Scholar*. He has taught at Columbia University and at Kent School. He is now living in Rome, where he is writing and is also on the faculty of St. Stephen's School.